ROUTLEDGE LIBRARY EDITIONS:
INDUSTRIAL RELATIONS

Volume 16

INDUSTRIAL ACTION

INDUSTRIAL ACTION

Patterns of Labour Conflict

Edited by
STEPHEN J. FRENKEL

Routledge
Taylor & Francis Group

LONDON AND NEW YORK

First published in 1980 by George Allen & Unwin

This edition first published in 2025
by Routledge
4 Park Square, Milton Park, Abingdon, Oxon OX14 4RN

and by Routledge
605 Third Avenue, New York, NY 10158

Routledge is an imprint of the Taylor & Francis Group, an informa business

© 1980 S.J. Frenkel

British Library Cataloguing in Publication Data
A catalogue record for this book is available from the British Library

ISBN: 978-1-032-81770-5 (Set)
ISBN: 978-1-032-84857-0 (Volume 16) (hbk)
ISBN: 978-1-032-84859-4 (Volume 16) (pbk)
ISBN: 978-1-003-51535-7 (Volume 16) (ebk)

DOI: 10.4324/9781003515357

Publisher's Note
The publisher has gone to great lengths to ensure the quality of this reprint but points out that some imperfections in the original copies may be apparent.

Disclaimer
The publisher has made every effort to trace copyright holders and would welcome correspondence from those they have been unable to trace.

Industrial Action
Patterns of
Labour Conflict

Edited by

STEPHEN J. FRENKEL

Sydney
GEORGE ALLEN & UNWIN
London   Boston

First published in 1980 by
George Allen & Unwin Australia Pty Ltd
8 Napier Street
North Sydney NSW 2060

National Library of Australia
Cataloguing-in-Publication entry:

Industrial action.
Index.
Bibliography.

ISBN 0 86861 122 0
ISBN 0 86861 130 1 Paperback
1. Labour disputes — Australia —

Case studies. I Frenkel, Stephen, ed.
331. 89'0994

Library of Congress
Catalog Card Number: 80-67730

Set in 10 on 11pt Plantin by Jacobson
Typesetters Ltd.
Printed in Hong Kong

Contents

Tables

Figures

Abbreviations

ABS	Australian Bureau of Statistics
AC&AC	Australian Conciliation & Arbitration Commission
ACOA	Administrative and Clerical Officers Association
ACTU	Australian Council of Trade Unions
AEU	Amalgamated Engineering Union
AMWSU	Amalgamated Metal Workers' and Shipwrights' Union
APSA	Australian Public Service Association (4th division Officers)
APTU	Australian Postal and Telecommunications Union
ASC&J	Amalgamated Society of Carpenters & Joiners
ASE	Australasian Society of Engineers
ATEA	Australian Telecommunications Employees Association
ATPOA	Australian Telephonists and Phonogram Officers Association
AWU	Australian Workers' Union
BLF	Australian Building Construction Employees and Builders' Labourers Federation
BTG	Building Trades Group
BWIU	Building Workers' Industrial Union of Australia
CIR	Commission on Industrial Relations
ETU	Electrical Trades Union of Australia
FEDFA	Federated Engine Drivers and Firemen's Association of Australasia
FIA	Federated Ironworkers Association of Australia
FMWU	Federated Miscellaneous Workers' Union of Australia
FSPDU	Federated Ship Painters and Dockers' Union of Australia
FSSCA	Federated Shipwrights and Ship Constructors' Association of Australia.
IAC	Industries Assistance Commission
JIC	Joint Industrial Council (Department of Defence)
MBA	Master Builders' Association of New South Wales
MBFA	Master Builders' Federation of Australia
MTIA	Metal Trades Industries Association
NZWEU	New Zealand Waterside Employers' Industrial Union of Employers
NZWWF	New Zealand Waterside Workers' Federation
NZWWU	New Zealand Waterside Workers' Union

OPDU	Operative Painters and Decorators Union
OPPWF	Operative Plasterers and Plaster Workers' Federation
OSSA	Operative Stonemasons Society of Australia
PGEU	Plumbers and Gasfitters Employees' Union of Australia
TWU	Transport Workers' Union
UPCT	Union of Postal Clerks and Telegraphists
WIC	Waterfront Industry Commission

Notes on Contributors

Stephen Frenkel MA Ind. Relations (Warwick) – Research Fellow, Industrial Relations Research Centre, University of New South Wales. Joint author of two recent books on British industrial relations entitled *Shop Stewards in Action* and *The Social Organization of Strikes.*

Alice Coolican B Com (Hons) UNSW – Research Assistant, currently working with Stephen Frenkel on a project focusing on comparative union organisation and militancy in the construction and metal industries.

Barry Muller M Com (UNSW) – research student at the University of New South Wales. Research interests include workplace industrial relations with special reference to the public sector.

Vic Taylor MA Ind. Relations (Warwick) – Senior Lecturer in Industrial Relations, Australian Graduate School of Management, University of New South Wales. He has published a number of papers on incomes policy and trade unionism and is currently engaged in research on redundancy and management approaches to industrial relations.

Don Turkington PhD (Victoria) – Senior Lecturer in Industrial Relations, Victoria University of Wellington. Author of a recent book entitled *Industrial Conflict.* Currently researching strikes in the coal mining industry and influences on collective bargaining in New Zealand.

Preface

A glance at the products and services available in any modern industrial society, or a visit to workplaces in different industries, is convincing enough evidence of great diversity. On the other hand there are the unifying tendencies generated by a shared economic system, government policies, the behaviour of tribunals, management, and unions. This book focuses on these conflicting themes by addressing the issue of industrial action; a problem of relevance to both academics and policy-makers alike.

In describing and examining industrial action in four industries, the contributors have made the task of comparative analysis easier by using a common analytical framework and mode of presentation.

The project has benefited from the help of many people. We wish to thank Mark Paul and Sheena Frenkel for arranging the seminar at which the papers included in this book were first presented. Thanks also to Joan Dillon, Joy Marsh, Karen Matthews and Felicity Simmons for typing various parts of the manuscript. Our special gratitude goes to the many trade union officials, managers, employers association officers and public servants who provided us with insights and information without which the project would not have been possible. Needless to say they bear no responsibility for the subsequent analyses.

Stephen J. Frenkel
University of New South Wales
February 1980.

CHAPTER ONE

Theory and Research Strategy*

Stephen J. Frenkel

Strikes and other forms of industrial action have long been a controversial feature of the Australian industrial landscape, and yet these collective challenges to industrial authority have seldom been examined in a systematic and detailed manner.[1] This book is intended as a corrective, limited though it may be in the size of its canvas. More specifically, the project is designed to explore the principal factors associated with industrial action in construction, shipbuilding and shiprepair, the waterfront, and the telecommunications industry. The study is perhaps better comprehended when placed in the wider context of current Australian industrial relations research.

The conciliation and arbitration system which dominates Australian industrial relations practice has given rise to numerous studies by lawyers and economists. There has been a tendency to regard the accommodation arrangements as either the source or − with some fine tuning − the solution to several fundamental economic and political problems. Perhaps because of the relevance of industrial relations to public and corporate policy, the academic status of the subject is continually threatened by a narrow pre-occupation with the efficacy of industrial law and concern with the effects of the arbitration system on wage determination, inflation, economic productivity, and unemployment.

We are not suggesting that the practical implications of industrial relations institutions and processes do not merit serious attention, what is being argued is that the hegemony of law and economics *vis-à-vis* academic research has had a number of adverse consequences. Ideas and insights from other disciplines such as sociology and psychology have been neglected, while comparatively few studies have been based on fieldwork research.[2] There has been a strong tendency to rely on official documentary material and statistics and to focus research on the formal attributes of industrial relations institutions and procedures. Although

---

*I would like to thank the contributors to this volume, Sheena Frenkel and Mark Paul for comments on earlier drafts of this chapter. However, responsibility for its contents lies solely with the writer.

studies of this kind have contributed significantly to our stock of knowledge they rarely convey the realities of industrial relations: the informal 'wheeling and dealing' and social networks that are essential lubricants in the system. Concentration on the formal mechanisms has also detracted from investigations into workplace industrial relations yet it is only by virtue of the existence of management and workers that industrial relations exist at all.

There is also a tendency (by no means confined to Australian scholars), to under-rate the importance of international comparisons in industrial relations. Typically, it is argued that issues requiring resolution are unique to Australia, or the socio-political context is alleged to be so different that comparative analysis is a pointless exercise. This kind of reasoning also leads to the conclusion that overseas theoretical debates have little relevance for the understanding of local industrial relations. The upshot of this is that theorising aimed at the clarification of ideas, the generation and integration of concepts, and the establishment of research priorities remains under-developed.

These critical observations must, however, be viewed in the light of rapidly changing circumstances. Indeed, there are four factors that are facilitating apparently significant changes in the nature of the academic study of industrial relations in Australia. Firstly, there are the clear similarities in the economic and industrial relations problems that advanced capitalist societies are currently facing. Secondly, there is the rapid dissemination of information, made increasingly possible by modern communications systems. Thirdly, there are a substantial number of Australian industrial relations academics who have been educated overseas. And fourthly, the total number of industrial relations scholars has risen appreciably in recent years. Taken together, these factors are promoting greater interest in alternative perspectives and overseas studies, including an appreciation of the benefits to be gained from examining Australian industrial relations in new ways.

This book reflects something of the change in focus and style of industrial relations research in Australia. Our approach is distinguished from most previous comparable studies by its emphasis on:

1. the development of theory based on empirical research;
2. the use of concepts drawn from a number of academic disciplines and perspectives;
3. a comparative standpoint both in relation to the shaping of a theoretical framework and with respect to analysis of the case study data;
4. the examination of industrial action patterns instead of statistical categories devised by official agencies for purposes other than industrial relations research.

These four features are elaborated further in the subsequent discussion, which summarises the analytical framework and research strategy underlying the project.

Theory and Research on Industrial Action

Official statistics in several countries reveal considerable variations in dispute incidence between industries (Australian Bureau of Statistics, Catalogue no. 6322.0; Department of Employment Gazette; Handbook of Labor Statistics). Although previous research indicates that there are certain factors of explanatory importance (McLean, 1979; Shorey, 1976; Smith *et al.*, 1978: 71-76; Turkington, 1976), there is at present no satisfactory theory of inter-industry labour conflict. There is then considerable theoretical justification for taking 'the industry' as the prime unit of analysis. This point is reinforced by several additional considerations. The first consideration is the predominance of awards and agreements relating to specific industries; the second is the tendency for employers to organise along product market lines (Plowman, 1978); the third is that the publication of much official socio-economic information is categorised on an industry basis; and the fourth is that the small size of workplaces with the concentration of decision-making power at the State branch or regional level of most unions means that it is sensible to focus research, at least initially, above the workplace level.

While unions, rather than industries, might have been chosen as the central analytical unit, this option has two distinct disadvantages. Available evidence suggests that factors associated with markets, technology, and the work process are more important than external union organisation in explaining worker militancy (Frenkel, 1978b; Turkington, 1976). Moreover, there are substantial practical research problems associated with a comparative study of occupational unions.[3] In any case it is possible to examine variations in union militancy in the context of a study focusing on inter-industry dispute patterns.

We will continue to use the terms industrial disputes and industrial action interchangeably. However, it is important to note that our definition is wider than that used by the official statistician (ABS, Catalogue no. 6322.0). Industrial action is taken to include all forms of overt, collective labour conflict irrespective of the number of man-days 'lost'. Accordingly, less reliance is placed on official categories and published statistics; rather an attempt has been made to develop empirical referents and assemble data most appropriate to the goals of the research project. Nevertheless, where practicable, we have tried to maintain comparability with official data coding practices.

The empirical categories or dimensions of industrial action used in the subsequent case studies can be summarised quite briefly.[4] These include the *form* in which conflict is expressed, that is, whether in strikes, bans or other types of overt collective action. *Frequency* and *working days 'lost'* give some idea of the incidence of industrial disputes. *Duration* indicates the depth of social organisation, or persistence of the parties, or both. *Organisational scope* is a measure of the scale or extent of social organisation involved on the labour side in industrial disputes. The *unions involved* tell us something about comparative union militancy; the *cited issues* suggest the precipitating causes of conflict. Taken in conjunction with each other, these measures yield a pattern or profile. This is a descriptive abstraction which permits comparative analysis of the deprivations, mobilisation capabilities, and social organisational characteristics of workers in different industries. The primary aim of the project is the discovery and explanation of similarities and differences in the industrial action patterns of the four industries referred to earlier.

In developing the theoretical framework, to be outlined shortly, three recent studies have had a significant influence on our thinking. These include Hugh Clegg's analysis of industrial disputes in six advanced capitalist societies, in which he demonstrated the importance of bargaining structures in accounting for variations in dispute patterns (1976: 68–82). It was further argued that these institutional arrangements were largely shaped by employers or the state.[5] At a more disaggregated level, Batstone, Boraston and Frenkel (1977) analysed the relationships between technology, work organisation, management control systems, and the social organisation of workers in a large British motor vehicle plant. This included a detailed, separate examination of strikes (Batstone *et al.*, 1978). Emphasis on the interplay between technology, work organisation, the nature of trade union organisation, and the capacity to utilise various forms of sanctions against management has also been discussed by Shorter and Tilly (1974: 174–187) in a significant contribution to the literature.

These studies suggest that the dominant industrial relations system in a society or industry and the nature of social relations at the point of production are likely to constitute the essential elements in an explanation of the industrial action pattern of one or more industries. This hypothesis has been explored by the writer in a number of earlier papers (Frenkel, 1978a; 1978c; 1979); here it is simply necessary to clarify the meaning of one of our central concepts and thereafter summarise the factors that it was thought essential to explore by means of empirical research.

The term *accommodation structure* will be used to denote certain key features of the industrial relations arrangements and processes in an industry (or society). These include:
1. The dominant mode of regulation, that is, whether procedural and substantive rules are shaped by collective bargaining, direct statutory

regulation, compulsory arbitration, or any other regulative mechanism. Two important aspects of the mode of regulation are the extent to which industrial action is legally permitted and the equity, or fairness, of the rules according to those responsible for their sanction. (Typically full time union officers amongst others).

2. The number of representative organisations involved in the accommodation process.
3. The number of primary or major awards, agreements, and statutes relevant to the industry.
4. The degree of formalisation denoted by awards or agreements, that is, the extent to which the primary regulative instruments are documented in detail and possess legal status.
5. The scope of awards or agreements refers to the number of different types of issues subject to joint regulation. The existence or otherwise of disputes procedures is worthy of note.
6. The extent to which the primary regulative instruments are forged at higher (more centralised) or lower organisational levels.

Accommodation structures are typically sustained by the interaction of the policies and power of the organisations involved in industrial relations. These include employers and their representative institutions, trade unions, and the state (typically statutory bodies and the courts). The strategies of the parties derive from many sources and take into account wider conditions associated with the political and economic context, nevertheless they must be applied to workplace problems. Accordingly, we believe it important to examine the influences on organisations that account for the nature of accommodation structures, the factors associated with workplace dynamics, *and* the dialectical relationship between these elements. The factors relevant to an empirical application of this conceptual model may now be outlined.

Employment relations in capitalist societies are mainly predicated on private ownership of the means of production and the operation of markets. Both the nature of ownership (whether private, state, or social) and the character of markets merit attention. The importance of the product market in industrial relations is well attested (Levinson, 1966; Turner *et al.*, 1967), but it is necessary to tease out the various dimensions of this concept. These include the extent of homogeneity, stability, size, pressure of demand, and competition. Homogeneity refers to the degree of standardisation or similarity between competing products; stability denotes the frequency and amplitude of market fluctuations. The remaining terms are self-explanatory.

The macro political-economic environment may be expected to influence the behaviour of the interest groups: the level of aggregate demand, the rate of inflation, and the measures taken by the state to stabilise the economy are some of the more important aspects impinging on industrial relations strategies.

In the examination of employers' structures and strategies, the number, size, and geographical distribution of enterprises and workplaces are likely to be significant (Ingham, 1974). In addition, the extent to which decision-making is centralised (i.e. whether corporations or employers' associations concentrate decision-making locally or nationally) is also liable to influence the nature of accommodation structures (Clegg, 1976: 118). Whether or not labour relations policies are standardised across the industry is also noteworthy. In particular, it is important to examine the ideology and cohesion of employers, including their political networks (Bendix, 1974; Ingham, 1974; Jackson and Sisson, 1976).

External labour markets may be expected to influence the strategies of employers (A. L. Friedman, 1977), trade unions (Levinson, 1966; Shorey, 1976), and the state (Martin, 1979: 88–121; Soskice, 1978: 221–246). The five dimensions noted in our discussion of the product market are equally applicable to the labour market. Indeed, empirically there is likely to be some relationship between the supply and demand for goods and services on the one hand and labour on the other (Turkington, 1976; Turner *et al.*, 1967). It is, therefore, imperative to explore the mediating strategies and rules created by management and unions in adjusting the impact of the product market on labour utilisation (W. Brown, 1973; B. Thomas and Deaton, 1978).

In examining the role of trade unions in relation to industrial action it is necessary to note their membership density, number, size, and geographical dispersion. The severity of inter-union competition and internal factionalism is likely to influence their power (Taylor, 1978; Gallie, 1978), while the locus of decision-making and control, that is to say the tendency towards concentration at the centre (national headquarters) or towards the periphery (regions or workplaces) will, in part, determine the role and effectiveness of full-time union leaders (Boraston *et al.*, 1975; A. Friedman, 1976; Roomkin, 1976). Last but not least, the ideology and political networks of trade union officials and activists may be expected to have a significant bearing on the strategies and tactics of these organisations, including the responses of employers and the state (Korpi, 1978).

In considering the role of the state, it is clear that governments and other statutory bodies are, within constitutional limits, capable of significantly affecting both the procedural and substantive rules that govern relationships not only between management and unions but also between industrial organisations generally. In addition, the state may legislate to regulate the internal procedures of these organisations and proscribe certain types of activity. Thus it is important to note the way in which the state intervenes in industrial relations, particularly in relation to accommodation structures (Crouch, 1977; Strinati, 1979).

Finally, at the level of the workplace, the composition (in terms of age, gender, ethnicity, religion, and occupation), geographical and social location, and size distribution of the labour force require analysis (Shorter and Tilly, 1974). And as suggested earlier, the character of workplace relations has been shown to depend a good deal on technology, work organisation, and management control systems. These factors are likely to affect the power of groups and the character of workplace union organisation (Batstone *et al.*, 1977; Beynon, 1973), although they are also conditioned by the accommodation structure and strategies of the relevant major industrial groups (Gallie, 1978).

Having outlined the variables thought to be worthy of investigation it may be useful to reiterate our basic theoretical position and enter several caveats. As a starting point, we tentatively assume that industrial action in any industry depends upon the accommodation structure (as shaped by the distribution of power between the major industrial interest groups, including the state) and factors impinging on management and workers at workplace level. It is the dialectical relationship between these aspects that empirical research can illuminate and thereby contribute towards a more thorough understanding of industrial action at an intermediate level of analysis. There are, however, two qualifications which it is important to stress at the outset. Firstly, the framework described above is a structuring device and not a precise theory, hence there is little to be gained by exploring interrelationships between the variables on an *a priori* basis. Rather we prefer to discover these in the course of our empirical investigations. Secondly, no purpose is served by reporting on those factors which, though included in our framework, appear to have little explanatory value. So in the subsequent chapters our analyses will be limited to those variables that are particularly germane to the understanding and explanation of industrial action.

Choice of Industries

The empirical application of the analytical framework outlined above requires that industries be reasonably unambiguous (and hence identifiable) and have experienced (and recorded) sufficient industrial disputes to permit generalisations to be made. In addition, research access should not be impeded, and there should be sufficient researchers available who are familiar with, and committed to, the type of research implied by the research strategy. Our choice of industries was finally decided by reference to the last two conditions.

The construction, shipbuilding and shiprepair, and telecommunications industries studied are Australian, while the study of the waterfront (variously known as stevedoring or the docks) is based on New Zealand materials. This does not prejudice comparative analysis, since the water-front in both countries is substantially different to other industries. Until 1977 in Australia, stevedoring was regulated by special legislation and a separate tribunal: this continues to be the case in New Zealand. Notwith-standing these differences, the general accommodation system in the two countries are in any case very similar: both are based ultimately on compulsory arbitration. Furthermore, in the period under review the two countries were experiencing common problems with conservative gov-ernments pursuing broadly similar economic and industrial relations strategies (Woods, 1979; Mitchell, 1979).

Despite an apparent diversity, the four industries to be examined shortly possess two features which make comparative analysis especially interesting. Each has a strike-prone reputation, and they span skilled and unskilled occupational groups, including members of what might be termed the 'old' and 'new' working class (Low-Beer, 1978: 1–22). The extent to which, for example, the telecommunication technicians differ fundamentally from watersiders or metal tradesmen in their industrial attitudes and actions is clearly relevant to recent theorising on the emergence of new forms of unionism (Shorter and Tilly, 1974; Mallet, 1975).

The Australian Industrial Relations and Political Economic Context: A Background Sketch

Bearing in mind the need to place the case studies in their wider institu-tional and social context, a very brief introduction to the conciliation and arbitration system is provided, together with several observations on economic and political conditions during the period when the research was undertaken (1979).

Australia is a federation of six states and two territories. The role of the Federal Government in industrial relations is restricted by a written Constitution. With the exception of the territories and the Federal public sector, where the Government is the employer, the Constitution only allows the Government to legislate for the purpose of conciliation and arbitration in relation to the prevention and settlement of industrial dis-putes (Australian Constitution sec.51: [XXXV]). Simplifying a good deal, the term industrial dispute has been interpreted by successive High Court decisions to include the more important inter-state, intra-union and inter-union conflicts while excluding managerial prerogative issues (Sorrel, 1979: 112–125). State governments have plenary powers but they are required to acknowledge the primacy of the Federal conciliation and arbitration system wherever there is an inconsistency between State and Federal law (Australian Constitution sec.109). In any case there is a strong tendency for the State tribunals and Wages Boards (Victoria and Tasmania) to follow the lead given by the Federal Australian Conciliation and Arbitration Commission (AC&AC) with respect to wage determination. The importance of the AC&AC is further attested by the fact that almost 40 per cent of the Australian workforce is under the jurisdiction of the Federal Tribunal, with most of the remainder having their wages and conditions regulated by about fifty other statutory bodies (ABS, Catalogue no.6315.0, 1974).

State and Federal governments appear to have played a greater role in industrial relations in Australia than in other advanced capitalist societies. The parameters within which the tribunals operate are circumscribed by the Constitution but are expressed in a complex body of statute law that details their functions. Governments may intervene in the more important award hearings before the tribunals. Partly because of government intervention in industrial relations and the constitutional uncertainty surrounding the role of the state, the Australian industrial relations system is especially vulnerable to legitimation problems arising from two particular sources.

In the first place the jurisdiction of the Federal Tribunal is frequently tested in the High Court. These challenges have usually resulted in decisions that sacrifice practical industrial relations considerations for legal precision (see Macken, 1974, especially Part 1). Secondly, successive governments have used the law as the principal method of controlling trade union behaviour. This has taken the form of legal sanctions aimed at the prevention of industrial action and legislation facilitating state regulation of the internal procedures of labour and employers' organisations. The latter point is particularly important for the conduct of union elections, and jurisdiction or membership coverage (Rawson, 1978: 44–67; Sorrell, 1979: 160–170 and 134–146).

The operation of the conciliation and arbitration system requires representative organisations of employers and employees. It is largely on account of registration that certain rights and obligations are conferred on the unions. Though it is possible to opt out of the system, unions have found it preferable to continue as registered organisations. It is mainly as a consequence of the encouragement given to registered unions that union density in Australia is comparatively high (Howard, 1977: 260–269; Rawson, 1978). In 1978, 57 per cent of the labour force were union members (ABS Catalogue no.6323.0, 1979). The accommodation system has also had a significant influence on union structure. In short, the inception of compulsory conciliation and arbitration procedures at the turn of the century effectively guaranteed the continuity of occupational unionism

(Clegg, 1976: 32). Governments have done little to promote union amalgamation, with the result that in 1978 it was estimated that there were 279 unions in Australia (ABS Catalogue no.6323.0, 1979). Many of these unions would be unlikely to survive without the protection afforded them by the legislation and adherence by the tribunals to the concept of comparative wage justice.[6]

Martin (1975: 32) has commented that the Australian industrial relations system is based on compulsion in two senses:

> The first, and most obvious, is that once an arbitration decision has been handed down in the form of an award its terms are legally binding on the employers and employees covered by it. The second, and most significant, is that either employers or trade unions can legally compel the other to deal with issues of common concern through the arbitration machinery simply by submitting such issues to an appropriate arbitration authority.

It would appear that the great majority of disputes are settled by way of conciliation and mutual consent (see for example, the Annual Reports of the President of the AC&AC) however, the most important wages decisions are largely determined by compulsory arbitration.

At present the general accommodation structure in Australia consists of three tiers. At the national level the Federal Tribunal engages in periodic hearings where nationwide increases in wages and conditions are awarded. These increases as well as others determined at lower levels are required to be within guidelines initially established by the Tribunal in April 1975 but subject to review from time to time. These tend to limit decisions at national level to wage adjustments that are related to, but need not necessarily fully reflect, recent price increases. This so-called National Wage Indexation procedure is supposed to be the primary method of regulating wage increases; however, there is also provision for industry or company level awards. This second tier is important in practice, more so at present than the third and lowest level: the workplace. 'Over-award' bargaining occurs in the larger establishments, but it is generally discouraged by employer associations, tribunals, and especially the Federal Government.

During 1978 the national unemployment rate averaged around 6.2 per cent while inflation had been reduced to approximately 7.8 per cent from its dizzy height of 17.6 per cent in early 1975. Most commentators nevertheless agreed that the economy was in recession with little sign of an early recovery. The conservative national government having entered office in late 1975 regarded the reduction of inflation as its first priority. This led to large cuts in public expenditure, control of the money supply, and an uncompromising attitude towards the labour movement. Control of wage increases continues to be an essential part of the Government's strategy. Integral to this is the curbing of union power which the Government attempted to ensure by the introduction of a series of draconian laws, which conservative State administrations in Queensland and West Australia were quick to applaud and supplement with similar statutes (Essential Services Act, 1979; Industrial Arbitration Act, 1979). Significantly, by the end of 1979 no government had persevered with legal proceedings against the unions, seemingly in recognition of past experience that penal sanctions tended to exacerbate rather than resolve industrial conflict. Instead, in 1979 the national government, in its zeal to stem what it viewed as excessive wage increases 'handed out' by tribunals in award and over-award hearings, turned its attention to the behaviour of the commissioners and amended the Conciliation and Arbitration Act. This led to a strong protest by the Tribunal members and judges but apparently to no avail, though it is doubtful whether the new provisions are constitutional.

Conclusions

This introductory chapter has sketched the rationale, concepts, and theoretical framework that form the basis of our research. The choice of industries was explained together with a brief note on the prevailing accommodation system and political-economic context. The stage is now set for the industry case studies. These follow a similar format, though the nature of the analyses has required a certain amount of improvisation. In the following chapter Alice Coolican and Stephen Frenkel explore the contours of industrial struggle in the New South Wales construction industry. Emphasis is placed on the way in which market competition and instability interact with the union and accommodation structures to produce a complex pattern of industrial action. In Chapter Two Vic Taylor introduces readers to the shipbuilding and shiprepair industry, in which sectionalist workplace struggles are a major feature of this declining sector. By contrast, Don Turkington's analysis of the waterfront industrial action pattern in the third chapter shows that the great majority of disputes are establishment-wide in scope. This, he argues, is explicable largely in terms of union structure and organisation. In the following chapter Barry Muller focuses on the comparative militancy of technicians in the telecommunications industry. The frequent use of bans is explained in terms of the conjunction of a particular management ideology and strategy and an occupational group accustomed to high discretion work roles. The final chapter is devoted to drawing the threads of the separate industry studies together with the intention of developing a theory of industrial action at the industry level. Several of the more important theoretical and practical industrial relations implications of this general analysis are discussed together with some suggestions for further research.

NOTES
1. Most of the Australian strike studies are referred to in Frenkel, 1978c.
2. See for example Isaac and Ford (eds), 1971.
3. Distributed across many industries with a great number of awards, how would one study the rank and file and their relationship to the leadership of an occupational union? This would be necessary if one were to say anything significant about comparative union militancy.
4. Most of these ideas have been set out in an earlier paper, (Frenkel and Coolican, 1979).
5. Clegg has recently applied these ideas most persuasively, though with qualification, in his discussion of the British strike pattern, (Clegg, 1979: 260-295).
6. This principle is used by the tribunals to ensure as far as possible that 'employees doing the same work for different employers or in different industries should by and large receive the same amount of pay irrespective of their employers or industry . . .' (Engineering Oil Industry Case 1970, 134 Commonwealth Arbitration Reports: 165).

CHAPTER TWO

Competition, Instability and Industrial Struggle in the New South Wales Construction Industry*

Stephen J. Frenkel and Alice Coolican

The New South Wales Construction Industry has a reputation for aggressive attitudes and militant behaviour. Newspaper headlines such as 'High rise row costs $533m', 'Building workers in rowdy court invasion' and 'Work resumes on Australia's tower of trouble' tend to reinforce the conventional wisdom.[1] There is, however, some evidence in support of the view that this industry is dispute-prone. During the prosperous years of the early seventies the construction industry's share of total disputes in New South Wales was more than double its share of employment. It was not simply the incidence but also the character of these conflicts that encouraged the media's attention. Green bans emerged as a new form of struggle; these were based on an alliance between particular unions and resident action groups in order to prevent the demolition of buildings deemed to have social or historical value.[2] This significant widening of industrial conflict to include social and political issues was also accompanied by other unconventional tactics associated with the Mundey—Owens leadership of the Builders' Labourers Federation (BLF). These included the cessation of concrete pours prior to completion, the destruction of building work undertaken by non-union labour and the operation of vigilante groups in the form of flying, and, occasionally over-zealous, pickets. The industry became noted for violence, and in 1971 the BLF was expelled from the Labor Council for disrupting a meeting of Council delegates. Subsequently, in 1974 the Federal Union (including the New South Wales Branch) was de-registered, but the Union secured re-registration in 1976. These events were associated with a high level of both intra-union and inter-union conflict involving the BLF. Ideological differences between union leaders, especially those

*The research on which this chapter is based was made possible by the Australian Research Grants Council.

of the BLF and the BWIU (Building Workers' Industrial Union of Australia, the major tradesmen's union) intensified these antagonisms.[3] However, by 1975 the boom was at an end and the number of strikes declined considerably; so much so that in recent years the construction industry could hardly be regarded as one of the most dispute-prone in the State (see Table 2.4).

Unfortunately the turbulent years of the early seventies, which clearly influenced the public's image of the industry, lie outside the scope of this chapter. Their complexity merits separate, detailed analysis. Here we shall be concerned mainly with the latter half of the decade, a period of severe recession. An outline of the construction industry is provided in the next section, followed by a description of industrial action using unpublished information collected by the Department of Employment and Industrial Relations.[4] In the third section the industrial action pattern is analysed. It is argued that interaction between the mode of production and accommodation structure has a strong influence on the form, frequency, duration, location, and issues that characterise industrial disputes. Furthermore, the organisational features of industrial action are explicable by reference to union structures and strategies which interact with key elements of the mode of production and the accommodation structure. In the concluding section the future prospects for institutionalising conflict in the construction industry are considered.

Key Characteristics of the Construction Industry

The construction industry refers to those firms engaged in the creation, renovation, and repair of dwellings, commercial, industrial, and community buildings including civil engineering projects. On account of union and award coverage, certain fixed establishments in the public sector (which employ carpenters) are also included in this definition.[5] Table 2.1 shows the relative size of the industry's sub-sectors. In value terms, housing is the largest sub-sector (37.2 per cent) followed by commercial–industrial buildings (27 per cent). As indicated in the table, private enterprise dominates the financing of both these areas of activity with government expenditure being relatively more significant in civil engineering (90.8 per cent) and community buildings (73 per cent).

Industrial relations in the housing sub-sector are excluded from the subsequent analysis on the grounds that no major strike has occurred for over fifteen years. Union density is not known, but estimates vary between 20 per cent and 50 per cent compared to about 75 per cent in the remaining sub-sectors. Virtually all work is undertaken on a sub-contract basis. The small size of work teams and the closer relationships between

TABLE 2.1

Share of construction (ready-to-starts) New South Wales, private and government sectors, by type of building for June Quarter 1978

Sector	Housing %	Commercial– Industrial %	Flats %	Civil Engineering %	Community %
Private	91.2	76.9	80.6	9.2	27.0
Government	8.8	23.1	19.4	90.8	73.0
Total	100	100	100	100	100
Total value ($M)	*88.0	63.7	19.6	36.8	28.2
% of total value	37.2	27.0	8.2	15.6	12.0

*All figures are expressed in constant million dollars as at March 1975.

Source: Cordell's *Quarterly Review of Construction*, June Quarter 1978, for Commercial-Industrial, Flats, Civil Engineering and Community figures. Housing figures are estimates based on data from official sources.

sub-contractors and their superordinates have been cited as the main reasons for the very low level of industrial action in the housing section of the industry. In the period 1976–78 just over 7 per cent of the total employed population in New South Wales were engaged in the construction industry (ABS Catalogue no.6201.1). This represents one third of the total Australian construction workforce.

TABLE 2.2

Average number of persons, by occupation, working on new buildings, New South Wales, for selected periods *

	Carpenters	Brick- layers	Paint- ers	Plumb- ers	Builders' Lab- ourers	Electric- ians	Others	Total
1947–51	14 092	3564	3041	3131	6383	1948	5 223	37 382
1970–74	17 283	7350	4048	5086	8822	3703	11 589	57 881
1976–78	10 567	4100	2567	3200	4700	2500	7 133	34 767

*The figures refer to contractors, sub-contractors, and wage earners and include persons working on dwellings, other buildings (including alterations and additions and repairs and maintenance to the value of $10 000 and over) carried out by builders of new buildings. Persons constructing roads, railways, bridges, or their own houses are excluded. In 1962 the scope of the definition of persons working was widened to include persons working on jobs where there was no major contractor responsible for the work.

Source: ABS, *Building and Construction*, Cat. no. 8705.0.

As Table 2.2 shows the present size of the labour force has not changed substantially in comparison with the 1947–51 period, although there was a small increase in the growth of construction occupations up to the peak of the post-war building boom in 1974. But, by contrast, the industry's output has increased five-fold in real value terms since 1947–51, (ABS, Catalogue no's 8701.0 and 8705.0). The table reveals that some groups — bricklayers, electricians, and plumbers — have fared better than others, but, overall, it is remarkable that so few persons are engaged in the industry given the massive increase in production over the long term. Technological change, in the form of new building materials (largely manufactured off-site), more efficient construction equipment and techniques, and the concomitant growth of specialised sub-contracting teams, has significantly reduced the growth rate of employment in the industry. The greater volume of work has not led to much growth in employment.

According to calculations based on official data, the *nature* of employment relationships is also changing. In 1962 the ratio of sub-contractors to wage earners working on new buildings was 1 to 4.8 in New South Wales. By 1978 it was 1 to 2.6 (ABS, Catalogue no.8701.0). Moreover, a recent enquiry into permanency in the building industry (*Inquiry into Employment in the Building Industry, 1975*) estimated that nearly half of all employees were employed by sub-contractors. Clearly, the simple employer-employee relationship is almost an anachronism in the construction industry.

In passing, it is also worth noting that the labour force is almost totally male but heterogeneous in ethnic composition. Approximately one-quarter of the workforce were born in non-English speaking countries. However, there are no substantial differences in the ethnic composition of the various trades (ABS, Catalogue no.2418.0, 1979).

The co-ordination of work processes in construction are such that the industry is amongst a small number that combine unit production (Woodward, 1965: 37–39) with large scale organisation. A unique design constitutes the basis for work organised in a sequential manner, with each trade completing its set of tasks according to a predetermined, but not inflexible, programme. Delays usually attract costly contract penalties.

Construction firms vary in size and organisational structure: the traditional builder usually employs less than five persons, relying a good deal on sub-contract labour. He may either buy land and build on his own account or tender for work on a 'price for the job' or 'lump sum' basis. There is considerable specialisation both within the industry generally and within sub-sectors according to size of projects, with companies rarely entering unfamiliar markets unless forced to do so by liquidity problems.

Large projects (i.e. those valued at a million dollars or more) are undertaken by a small number of large companies many of whom offer design and management expertise. A typical arrangement is one where a contract is secured by tender with the price providing for building costs or both building and design costs. A more recent form of organisation, known as project management, shifts the financial risk from the construction company to the client. Under this arrangement, the design and managerial skills are leased by the client, either for a fixed fee or on a percentage of final cost basis. Unlike the conventional client–builder relationship, it is the company providing the finance that risks the final price of the project being outside expected limits.

There are several characteristics of management organisation and practice that have implications for the conduct of industrial relations. There is a relatively high concentration of production and employment in the industry. The only available data relates to Victoria, but we have no reason to believe that a similar picture does not apply to New South Wales. The *Inquiry into Employment in the Building Industry* estimated that 6.8 per cent of firms employing 150 employees or more accounted for 49.1 per cent of workers, while at the other end of the size scale 42.8 per cent of firms with less than 10 persons employed only 5.2 per cent of the wage-earning labour force. Despite this tendency towards concentration, the construction industry is highly competitive in all sub-sectors. Approximately two-thirds of construction work (in value terms) is subject to tendering, with all government contracts secured through this process (Cordell, 1979: 500–506).

A further feature of management organisation is the small proportion of permanent manual workers employed by construction companies. Most work is done by the contract system. This means that management must select contractors and sub-contractors, usually on a highly competitive price–reputation basis. A premium is placed on organisational skills since work must be efficiently sequenced and executed with minimum delay while simultaneously ensuring that the various professional stake-holders are satisfied. On a large project these include the design team, surveyors, engineers, government inspectors, and union officials. Hence a prime characteristic of construction management is the emphasis placed on what might be termed continuous negotiated brokerage. This, in turn, necessitates a high degree of informality, trust, and dependence on specialised professional knowledge. In short, project managers are required to co-ordinate various, relatively independent, technical and occupational groups within a highly constrained time frame.

The highly competitive and specialised nature of the construction industry is reflected in the institutions which seek to regulate relationships between contractors and workers. According to employer association officials, less than 40 per cent of eligible building employers (excluding those in housing and civil engineering) are members of the major employer organisation in the state (the Master Builders* Association of New South Wales). But most of these non-member firms are very small, indeed the same officials maintain that in value terms about 90 per cent of the work undertaken in the State is contracted by MBA members. Companies specialising in the civil engineering sub-sector are represented separately by the Australian Federation of Construction Contractors in matters of national industrial relations significance. For the purposes of advice, information, and dispute handling, civil engineering companies rely on the Employers' Federation of New South Wales; an association whose membership in industry terms is very diverse indeed.

In addition to these major associations, which are either branches of national organisations or affiliates of national employer bodies, there are a host of further organisations representing specialised contractors whose commercial interests are often in conflict with those of the main contractor. Apart from the Metal Trades Industries Association, organisations such as the Master Painters, Decorators and Signwriters Association of New South Wales, the Master Plumbers and Sanitary Engineers Association of New South Wales, and the Master Slaters, Tilers and Shinglers Association of New South Wales play a negligible role in industrial relations. They are mainly concerned with protecting the commercial interests of their members in the construction industry.

Although there are definite trends towards centralisation and unification among employers,[6] the hallmarks of their representative institutions remain fragmentation and local autonomy. These same features are suggested by Table 2.3 which gives an overview of the unions. There are several labour organisations with a majority of their members employed in the construction industry. In contrast to these *principal unions* there are others, some of which are large by Australian standards, whose construction members represent only a small minority of total membership; these are termed the *peripheral unions*. The most striking feature shown in the table is the large number of labour organisations associated with the construction industry. Many of these are craft unions, as suggested by their titles. Attention is also drawn to the numerical dominance of the BWIU, a fact of considerable significance for our subsequent analysis. Also worth noting is that in the period under review all the principal unions were members of the Building Trades Group (BTG), with the exception of the BLF which was re-admitted in 1979. The BTG is an inter-union body formally constituted under the New South Wales Labor Council rules.[7] Where it is deemed appropriate other unions may also be invited to participate in meetings.

Trends towards centralisation and unification on both sides of the industry have been accelerated by the creation in 1975 of the two major national construction awards. The National Building Trades Construction Award and the Building Construction Employees and Builders' Labourers Award, cover all tradesmen and semi-skilled workers respectively, with the exception of the electricians, plumbers, and skilled metal workers whose wages and conditions are regulated by separate State and national awards. Semi-skilled labourers working in the civil engineering sub-

TABLE 2.3

New South Wales State branch membership of unions associated with the construction industry, 1978

Principal Unions	* Building Workers' Industrial Union	BWIU	16 474
	* Operative Plasterers and Plaster Workers Federation	Plasterers	2 311
	* Operative Stonemasons Society of Australia	Stonemasons	460
	Plumbers and Gasfitters Employees Union	Plumbers	6 909
	Amalgamated Society of Carpenters & Joiners	ASC&J	2 320
	Operative Painters and Decorators Union	Painters	7 804
	** Australian Building Construction Employees & Builders' Labourers Federation	BLF	9 000
Peripheral Unions	Amalgamated Metal Workers and Shipwrights' Union	AMWSU	56 095
	Federated Engine Drivers and Firemen's Association	FEDFA	6 000
	Electrical Trades Union	ETU	28 303
	** Australian Workers' Union	AWU	27 000

*The Plasterers and Stonemasons have a working agreement with the BWIU which is virtually a *de facto* amalgamation.
**These figures are estimates derived from union officials. The AWU figure refers only to the General branch.

Source: Industrial Registrar of New South Wales, unpublished data.

sector are covered by the AWU (Australian Workers' Union) which is a major party to the General Construction and Maintenance, Civil and Mechanical Engineering etc. (State) Award.

In broad terms there are several features of the accommodation structure worth emphasising. Firstly, it is a complex set of legal arrangements, which nevertheless permits some scope for joint regulation by employers and unions. Secondly, most of the awards prescribe total earnings rather than minimum rates. These so-called paid rates awards have been subject to national wage indexation decisions since April 1975. Thirdly, despite some overlap between union coverage and the industry, at least in regard to the principal unions, these organisations are nevertheless parties to numerous awards and agreements, many of which lie outside the construction industry. The BWIU, for example, is respondent to about forty awards, and numerous formal and informal agreements. The trade unions are therefore forced to give priority to certain awards and agreements. This is encouraged by the institutionalisation of 'flow-ons', whereby increases in certain key award rates lead to similar increases in other awards.[8] By implication, union leaders must be thoroughly acquainted with the dynamics of award structures, and the components of awards if they are to maximise the gains to their total membership.

The industry's products, occupational profile, and organisational features associated with management and unions have been sketched: the characteristics of industrial struggle will now be examined.

Patterns of Industrial Action in the New South Wales Construction Industry

The following discussion is divided into two parts: first the general features of industrial action will be described. These include the form, frequency, duration, location, and issues precipitating collective action. The second part concentrates on the organisational attributes of industrial disputes. Unless otherwise stated all the dispute data discussed below refer to the three year period 1976–78.[9]

The General Characteristics of Industrial Action

Strike action appears to be the most common industrial tactic in Australia; the New South Wales construction industry is no exception, with 81 per cent of disputes involving strike activity, with 13 per cent taking the form of bans, and the remaining 6 per cent involving lost time due to unauthorised stop-work meetings.

Although data inadequacies make it impossible to rank the construction industry relative to other New South Wales industries in terms of dispute incidence, it is possible to gauge its share of disputes in relation to its relative size of employment. Table 2.4 contrasts the most recent period with that of the earlier boom years.

TABLE 2.4

Employment and industrial disputes in construction as a percentage of all industries, New South Wales, for selected years

	Average persons employed %	Average working days 'lost' %
1971–74	8.3	26.8
1975–78	7.8	8.1

Source: ABS Computer File, ABS, *The Labour Force New South Wales Feb. 1979* Cat. no. 6201.1 and ABS, *Industrial Disputes* Catalogue no. 6322.0.

It is plain that working days 'lost' relative to employment has declined markedly since the 1971–74 period. Indeed, since 1975 the construction industry has been no more dispute-prone than might be expected from its share of employment.

Within a certain range the duration of strikes in construction is bi-modal: 56 per cent lasted three days or less, and 37 per cent continued for five days or more. Stop-work meetings are characteristically short, all of these lasting less than a day. By contrast, 83 per cent of bans persisted for ten days or more.

Most industrial disputes occurred in urban areas. Some 71 per cent were concentrated in the Sydney metropolitan area with a further 14 per cent in other highly populated urban centres. Rural districts accounted for the remaining 15 per cent. With regard to sub-sectors: 69 per cent of disputes were reported to have taken place in the commercial–industrial building sector and 24 per cent on civil engineering projects. Fixed establishments employing maintenance tradesmen accounted for the remaining 7 per cent.

Fifty-nine per cent of disputes occurred in the private sector with the remaining 41 per cent taking place on projects financed by the State or Federal Government. There was considerable concentration of industrial action in certain companies: 36 per cent of the firms that reported conflicts experienced more than one dispute. These firms accounted for 68 per cent of all disputes. The most dispute-prone 5 per cent of companies, which experienced ten or more disputes, were responsible for 27 per cent of all labour conflicts. Notwithstanding the lack of accurate information, it should be borne in mind that the companies that reported one or more incidents of conflict form a very small proportion of the total number of operating construction firms in New South Wales.

The issues reportedly precipitating industrial action are presented in Table 2.5.

TABLE 2.5

Cited issues in construction industry disputes, New South Wales 1976–78

Cited Issue	%	%
Wages, Conditions and Benefits		30
Wage claims	22	
Conditions and benefits claims	8	
Management Behaviour		29
Dismissals	18	
Attitudes and actions	11	
Conciliation and Arbitration		22
Award claims	11	
Award interpretation	7	
Dissatisfaction with decisions	4	
Union Principles		12
Solidarity	6	
Demarcation	6	
Social Political		5
Other		2
Total		100
Number of disputes		227

Source: Weekly Reports, Department of Employment and Industrial Relations.

Wages, conditions, and benefits claims (30 per cent) together with management behaviour (29 per cent) account for nearly two-thirds of all disputes. Conciliation and arbitration processes also appear to precipitate a substantial number of conflicts (22 per cent) while social and political issues are much less significant (5 per cent).

This completes our description of the general features of industrial action in the construction industry. We now identify the organisational configurations associated with the struggles in which various types of unions are engaged.

The Organisational Attributes of Industrial Action

It is helpful to think of industrial disputes in terms of three dimensions: union involvement, level of instigation, and organisational scope. These dimensions refer respectively to the number of unions taking part in any industrial conflict, the extent to which the dispute is orchestrated at the workplace or at the union leadership level, and whether it embraces one or more workplaces. Unfortunately the Weekly Reports are not sufficiently detailed to allow any further elaboration. Table 2.6 summarises the eight main ideal types of industrial action based on these three dimensions.

TABLE 2.6

Types of industrial action

Union Involvement	Level of instigation	Organisational scope	Types of industrial action
Single union	workplace	single	autonomous
	workplace	multi	single union co-ordinated
	leadership	single	single union restricted campaign
	leadership	multi	single union campaign
Multi-union	workplace	single	domestic
	workplace	multi	multi-union co-ordinated
	leadership	single	multi-union restricted campaign
	leadership	multi	multi-union campaign

Autonomous disputes involve only one union, they are instigated by job delegates, or workers, or both and are confined to a single workplace. *Domestic* actions are similar to the former except that these involve more than one union. *Co-ordinated* disputes may be single or multi-union, their distinguishing features are that they are instigated at workplace level and embrace more than one establishment. Likewise *restricted campaigns* may include one or more unions, but these are orchestrated by union leaders external to the workplace yet they are confined to a single workplace. Finally, *campaigns* may be undertaken by the leadership of one or more unions; these disputes embrace more than one workplace.

All of these types of struggles occur in the construction industry but Table 2.7 shows that autonomous and domestic disputes are the most common.

TABLE 2.7

*Types of industrial action in the construction industry,
New South Wales, 1976–78*

Types of industrial action	%
Autonomous	46
Single union co-ordinated	3
Single union restricted campaign	9
Single union campaign	9
Domestic	25
Multi-union co-ordinated	1
Multi-union restricted campaign	1
Multi-union campaign	6
Total	100
Number of disputes	227

Source: Weekly Reports, Department of Employment and Industrial Relations.

Almost half of labour conflicts (46 per cent) are autonomous, and a further quarter (25 per cent) are domestic in nature. It should not go unnoticed that just over two-thirds (67 per cent) of all disputes are single union skirmishes. However, it is also worth bearing in mind that lack of data precluded an analysis based on working days 'lost'; we believe that a breakdown of that kind would illustrate the greater importance of multi-union disputes, especially campaign actions which, though typically short in duration, involve many construction workers, occasionally throughout the State.

Our first hand acquaintance with the industry suggested that unions not only vary in their propensity to engage in industrial struggle they also differ in the kinds of tactics which they employ. Data presented in Table 2.8 groups unions into five categories: the Labourers (BLF and AWU), the BWIU, the Craft organisations (Plasterers, Stonemasons, Plumbers, ASC&J, and Painters), the Mixed Peripheral unions (the AMWSU and FEDFA) and the Craft Peripheral group which only includes the ETU. The table indicates variations in the dispute patterns of the different union groups. These may be described in turn.

THE LABOURERS PATTERN – Both the BLF and AWU organise unskilled workers in the construction industry: the former on building sites and the latter in the much smaller civil engineering sub-sector. Members of these unions are mainly involved in autonomous (42 per cent), and to a lesser extent domestic (30 per cent), disputes. Although not discernible in Table

TABLE 2.8

*Types of action by unions in the construction industry,
New South Wales, 1976–78*

Types of industrial action	Union Patterns of Industrial Action				
	Labourers	BWIU	Craft	Peripheral	
				Mixed	Craft
	%	%	%	%	%
Autonomous	42	25	9	26	14
S U *co-ordinated	4	–	3	5	–
S U restricted campaign	14	–	–	1	–
S U campaign	8	9	3	–	14
Domestic	30	47	10	54	29
M U *co-ordinated	2	2	1	1	–
M U restricted campaign	–	1	7	–	–
M U campaign	–	16	67	13	43
Total	100	100	100	100	100
Number of disputes **	138	81	69	65	14

*S U and M U are abbreviations for single union and multi-union respectively.
** Since unions are taken as the unit of measurement, multi-union disputes necessarily involve double counting. The total number of disputes is, therefore, greater than their real number as reported in other tables.

Source: Weekly Reports, Department of Employment and Industrial Relations.

2.8, BLF members engage in many more single union restricted campaign and campaign struggles (31 per cent of that union's total disputes) than the AWU (6 per cent).

THE BWIU PATTERN – The BWIU organises skilled and semi-skilled workers, mainly in the construction industry. In contrast to the Labourers' unions dispute profile, two-thirds (65 per cent) of disputes in which BWIU members are involved are multi-union struggles. The majority of these are domestic conflicts, which account for 47 per cent of the union's total number of disputes. Significantly, the BWIU took part in all campaigns during the three-year period even though these only accounted for 16 per cent of the union's total conflicts. Autonomous actions are also relatively common (25 per cent).

THE CRAFT PATTERN – The five principal craft unions included in this group have a comparatively small membership and seldom engage in industrial action. With the exception of the Plumbers, when they are involved in disputes it is almost invariably with other unions (85 per cent) especially in multi-union campaigns (67 per cent).

THE MIXED PERIPHERAL PATTERN – Members of the AMWSU (Amalgamated Metal Workers' and Shipwrights' Union) and FEDFA (Federated Engine Drivers and Fireman's Association of Australia), unions which organise skilled and semi-skilled workers in the construction industry (and in most others), tend to engage in domestic (54 per cent) and, to a lesser extent, autonomous disputes (26 per cent). These unions also take part in some significant campaigns although this is not self-evident from the table.

THE CRAFT PERIPHERAL PATTERN – The ETU (Electrical Trades Union of Australia) is a craft union, the bulk of whose membership lies outside the construction industry. Like the Plumbers, electricians tend to be more prepared to take industrial action than their craft union counterparts, although in a similar vein, a large proportion of disputes in which they are involved are multi-union campaigns (43 per cent). Domestic struggles account for most of the remainder (29 per cent).

Having presented both the general industrial action profile and those pertaining to the particular union groups we shall now attempt to explain these findings. But first some brief theoretical remarks.

The Interpretation of Industrial Action

Our explanation is cast largely in terms of two concepts: the mode of production and the accommodation structure. The latter requires no elaboration since the meaning of this concept has been clarified in the first chapter (p.15). By mode of production we refer to the key features of the production system: ownership and control, markets, technology, and the labour process. The construction industry is characterised by a particular mode of production, which has an important bearing on dispute patterns.

As noted earlier, there is a certain dualism in the structure of the industry. A small number of large, privately owned enterprises operate both in conjunction, and in competition, with many more smaller units. Competition in the product market is in fact very keen. In terms of technology and the labour process, building is a labour-intensive activity of a unit or product-specific kind (Woodward, 1965: 35–49). Specialised work teams perform particular tasks according to a tightly monitored cost and time programme. Profit maximisation is facilitated less by increased direct supervisory control and more by the encouragement given to self-regulating teams of contract workers, made possible by construction technology (Stinchcombe, 1959). The work setting tends to be more hazardous, and tasks are frequently more arduous, than in comparable jobs.[10] Although there are variations in the duration of contracts, depending on the size and complexity of the project, the construction cycle is of short duration. This implies that workers in this industry must be highly mobile between building sites.

Explaining the General Features of Industrial Action

The finding that strikes are the dominant form of collective action in the construction industry evokes a simple explanation: it is the customary mode of expressing discontent because union officials much prefer strikes and court demonstrations to black bans. This may well be true, but does this merely reflect tradition *per se* or does it rather imply that strikes are strategically the most effective sanction against employers? Our field research suggest that strikes are generally the most effective tactic, given the high premium placed by management on building within a specific period. Workers and union officials also prefer immediate answers to their claims: the decision-making process is generally hastened by strike action. Bans tend to be less effective.

A little more can be said about the use of bans. Bans tend to be applied as an initial test of strength or as an alternative to strike action, especially where membership support for a complete withdrawal of labour is problematic. The little evidence we have suggests that bans are used as an alternative to strike action in at least three further types of circumstance: where one or more unions prefer to limit the intensity of conflict, as often happens in demarcation disputes; where sanctions are aimed at a third party with a view to furthering the goals of the organisation(s), but without immediate benefit to the rank and file; or where strikes are less effective, as in the case of green bans, where the aim is to prevent work from commencing on certain designated sites.

Fifty two per cent of all bans in the period 1976–78 were imposed by the BLF while over 80 per cent of these were single union actions. This is perhaps explicable by reference to the higher than average job mobility of builders' labourers relative to other construction workers (Inquiry into Employment, 1975: 16). Because of high turnover, it is easier for union officials to implement and police a total ban on a particular site than it is to wage organised çampaign struggles among a transient workforce.

Turning from the form to the frequency of industrial action it appears that managers in each period perceived market competition to be increasing relative to the previous quarter (ANZ Bank Quarterly, Surveys of Construction Activity, 1978). This broad sentiment was corroborated in interviews with forty-one construction managers: 78 per cent cited competition, lack of work, or low profit margins as the major current problem facing their company. According to several respondents, cash flow problems had been further exacerbated by construction firms moving out of their traditional, specialised areas of the market in search of work. Large firms were tendering for smaller projects and vice versa.

Keen competition contributes significantly to the instability of construction enterprises. On the basis of official data, it was estimated that in

1978 construction firms had a failure rate six times greater than the State average.[11] Market competition and enterprise instability may be expected to have significant implications for industrial relations.

The effects of the product market can best be understood through an appreciation of the particular form which it assumes in this industry: the tendering system. Whether tenders are by open or selected competition (the two main variants), the successful (sub-) contractor is likely to have offered the lowest price or shortest contract time at a competitive price. Similarly, there is pressure for maximum efficiency under project management where reputation depends, amongst other things, on effective cost control. The industrial relations implications of market pressure manifested in 'tight' tendering and managerial sensitivity is neatly summed up by a leading industrial relations manager as follows:

> So, in a nutshell, most builders today are working to prices based on an optimistic assessment of risk with little margin for profit. It is a perfect recipe for inflexibility in industrial [relations] matters and a huge temptation to seek to avoid legal and moral obligations which cost money. (Lovell, 1979: 57)

The priority given to production and profit by construction managers was evident from our interviews: 92.7 per cent of respondents referred to building within time and budget limits and hence making a profit or retaining market share as their main objective at site level. By contrast, when asked to list their priorities less than 1 per cent of respondents mentioned improvements in labour relations. Of particular interest, however, are the results of the quarterly surveys referred to earlier (p.38). These demonstrate that managers anticipated the increasing cost of labour as being one of the main constraints on profitability. Managers, therefore, were apparently subject to conflicting market pressures: on the one hand, the product market required cost containment and, on the other, cost increases were emanating from the labour market. With the emphasis placed on the former it follows that labour pressure was to be strongly resisted, while simultaneously encouraging maximum effort for minimum labour input. The translation of product market constraints to the labour process is reflected in the accelerated increase in the use of sub-contract labour and covert expressions of conflict. Thus, when the managers surveyed were asked about their major labour problems 65 per cent of responses were couched in terms of low workforce morale and high levels of absenteeism. This suggests the possibility that workers were resorting to covert strategies, such as output restriction and absenteeism, in order to maintain what they perceived to be an equitable wage-work bargain.[12] This hypothesis is made more plausible if it is possible to find empirical evidence for workers' awareness of conflict with management co-existing with a reluctance to engage in overt collective struggle. While we have no direct information on rank and file workers' attitudes, evidence from sixty-seven completed job delegate questionnaires is quite conclusive.[13] Presented with a forced choice question on their image of management, 72 per cent agreed that 'most employers try and get as much out of the workers as possible so you have to struggle for many of the things you want', while the remaining 25 per cent (excluding the 3 per cent who failed to answer) believed that 'most employers treat their workers fairly'. This conflict consciousness was not matched by any zeal for collective action. Thus, in response to a question concerning the two most difficult problems faced by job delegates, 55.3 per cent referred to member apathy, problems associated with collection of dues, and lack of unity on the site. The low level of members' responsiveness apparently affected job delegates' relations with management; management behaviour accounted for 25 per cent of steward problems. These included managements' general lack of concern for workers' needs, insufficient answers to claims, and allegations of victimisation.

Workers were probably also restrained in their actions by the barrage of government and media propaganda, which sought to discredit trade unions by attributing the current economic recession to excessive wage demands. One union organiser remarked:

> I don't think the legislation [changes to the Arbitration Act] has had the effect – it's the propaganda that went before and after the legislation that did something. You go on site and you hear all Street's [Minister for Industrial Relations] propaganda quoted back at you – it's the unions doing everything –causing strikes . . .

Certainly this was a common view expressed by union officials in the construction industry. On the other hand, there were limits to workers' acquiescence. This is indicated in job delegates' assessments of their members' current willingness to engage in a national construction strike in order to *defend* their wages and conditions. Fifty-seven per cent believe their members would respond 'extremely favourably' while a further 21 per cent thought they would be 'very favourably' disposed to a call for action. By contrast, the responses to a similar question relating to *improvements* in wages and conditions yielded responses of 28.4 per cent and 17.9 per cent respectively. The available evidence suggests then that most construction workers were unwilling to engage in collective action to improve wages and conditions presumably preferring to respond informally and covertly. Nevertheless, they were prepared to counter any co-ordinated employer's offensive. But why were workers reluctant to take industrial action at a time of falling real wages? The key to understanding this lies in their generally weak labour market position.

The relationship between registered unemployment and vacancies in the New South Wales construction industry over recent years is presented in Table 2.9.

TABLE 2.9

Registered unemployed persons and vacancies in the New South Wales construction industry, 1976–78

Year	Unemployed	Vacancies	U/V ratio
1976	5714	146	39.1
1977	5513	217	25.4
1978	5089	260	19.6

Source: Monthly Review of the Employment Situation, Department of Employment and Industrial Relations, June 1976–78.

Although there appears to be a slight improvement in the demand for labour since 1976, the general situation is characterised by massive unemployment. Even in 1978 there were almost twenty persons registered as unemployed for every one vacancy. This is certainly not the most favourable context in which to mount actions for the improvement of workers' living standards.

Apart from the influence of the labour market on workers' perceptions, there are several further factors which contributed to the comparatively low incidence of disputes between 1976 and 1978. Some of these are associated with the mode of production, while others are consequences of the accommodation system.

There is some evidence (discussed below p.43) that suggests that industrial disputes tend to be concentrated on large sites. All other things being equal, a decline in the proportion of large sites will facilitate a reduction in the frequency of conflict. We were unable to find data relating to changes in the demand for, and hence supply of, large buildings, but when asked about this, a leading union official remarked:

> There definitely has — I've got no figures to prove it but in 1973–74 during the boom we used to have two organisers in the city [Sydney]. There would have been forty big buildings going up just in the city centre. Now we have halved our workforce — there's only work for one organiser in the city — probably only a dozen big buildings going up at the moment.

Clearly, the changing composition of demand in the product market is intimately related to the general decline in the economy since the early seventies. A State Labor Government has, however, been persuaded to make good at least some of the shortfall in private and national government expenditure in the construction industry. Data concerning the amount of building expenditure in the Sydney region (more comprehensive information being unavailable) by government source are shown in Table 2.10.

TABLE 2.10

Current value of 'ready-to-start' construction in the Sydney region by Government sector

June Quarter	Federal Government $ million	State Government $ million	Local Government & utilities $ million	Total $ million	State Government %
1976	10	12	8	30	40.0
1977	3	23	9	35	65.7
1978	10	39	6	55	70.9

Source: Cordell's, *Quarterly Review of Construction.*

It is plain that while Federal Government spending in New South Wales has declined in real terms since the present Government took office in December 1975, that of the State Government has increased dramatically, so much so that in 1978 the State Government's contribution was almost four times that of the national administration. Although there has been no explicit social contract between the unions and the State Government, an exchange relationship exists in the sense that unions are prepared to take some responsibility for ensuring the continuity of a Labor administration so long as the Government is fulfilling its obligations to the labour movement (Korpi and Shalev, 1979). As one senior left wing union official remarked: 'We'd try very much not to adversely affect the election chances of a Labor government, if it is progressive . . .'

The effects of awards and the processes of conciliation and arbitration on industrial conflict are, like the conflict of government–union relations, difficult to assess. But we believe that the existence of paid rates awards, which were indexed shortly after their creation in 1975, left most building workers with some sense of justice in regard to inter-occupational relativities.[14] Furthermore, although the existence of the AC&AC (Australian Conciliation and Arbitration Commission) paradoxically invites disputes, several that we observed would have been substantially prolonged but for the mediating skills of the relevant commissioners.

Finally, reference should be made to the substantial gains which the building unions achieved between 1970 and 1975.[15] These were likely to have dampened expectations of further successes, while in the case of the BLF, the new State branch leaders came into office with virtually no organisational resources; they were compelled to build and consolidate their union. And so it can be argued that the relatively low incidence of disputes in the period is partly a consequence of reduced expectations by unions that had made substantial gains in the previous period and the organisational imperatives placed on the BLF following the demise of its previous branch leadership.

Considering the third general dimension of industrial action, namely duration, it is easy to understand why bans tend to be applied for lengthy periods. From earlier remarks, it is plain that the impact of bans is generally less severe than strikes, so that they must be applied for longer periods. Stop-work meetings, on the other hand, are concluded in a relatively short time, since these are essentially forums for the endorsement of proposals, though some discussion does take place. Stop-work meetings generally occur during lunch or tea breaks, and lost time is recorded when these over-run the time authorised by the relevant award or agreement.

The bi-modal distribution of strikes is more difficult to explain. We calculated that 75 per cent and 64 per cent of multi-union and single union campaign stoppages respectively last less than one day. This accords with our observation that union leaders are keen to make a show of strength in award negotiations, yet at the same time avoid signs of weakness that might become visible if such widespread actions begin to attract oppposition from less committed members. Furthermore, and this applies to strikes of various kinds, the early hearing of disputes by tribunal members means that there is less incentive to persevere with sanctions (Holden, 1967), unless, of course, the conciliated settlement or determination is unacceptable to the workers. On such rare occasions, short duration protest actions take place. The more protracted disputes, those lasting five days or more, tend to be autonomous (57 per cent) or domestic disputes (30 per cent). It will be recalled that the common denominators of these two types of industrial action are worker mobilisation, which occurs without planning and orchestration from union headquarters, and the confinement of conflict to a single workplace. This suggests that these disputes represent trials of strength between work groups or workplace union organisations and management.

As regards the location of industrial action, it is clear that most disputes occur in the three metropolitan centres, simply because 72 per cent of the industry's workforce is concentrated in these areas (ABS, *Population and Dwellings*, 1976, Catalogue no.2427.0).

The roughly equal distribution of disputes in the private and public sectors may seem to be inconsistent with the notion that a political exchange relationship between the trade unions and the State Government reduces industrial conflict. For if that is so why are there not fewer disputes on government jobs? There are several reasons for this. Firstly, autonomous and domestic actions frequently focus on job-specific issues: organisers cannot easily dissuade the men from taking action, and indeed there is little incentive to do so. A small strike, after all, cannot seriously affect the position of the government. Secondly, and more importantly, although the State Government does undertake some construction work, the great majority of its projects are managed by private companies, so from the unions' and workers' point of view, industrial action is directed not at the Government but at the managing company. There is, nevertheless, one large community project where disputes have been less common than they might otherwise have been as a result of good relationships between the State Government, the unions, and the construction company.

A third reason for the similar number of disputes in the private and public sectors is simply that large projects (valued at over $1 million) tend to be equally distributed between the two sectors. The only available data, which is restricted to the Sydney region, indicates that, in 1978, 46.3 per cent of large projects were undertaken in the public sector, which in turn experienced 40 per cent of the total number of disputes in that year.

The tendency for industrial action to be concentrated in a relatively small number of companies is associated with their considerably greater incidence on large construction sites. Analysis of the Weekly Reports show that twenty-nine sites accounted for 79 per cent of industrial disputes. As far as we have been able to ascertain all these sites involved projects costing more than one million dollars. This does not mean that *all* large sites are dispute-prone; we simply do not have the data to draw such a conclusion. However, interview materials support the hypothesis that disputes are more likely on large sites. The following comments are from a union official and manager respectively:

> The issues of the industry are fought out where there is a concentration of production, employment, and power and this determines the standard of the industry. Our policy is to use power on big sites to benefit members as a whole.

> The BLF had a campaign of hitting the big sites. The union organisers would come at least twice a week. They'd know the delegates pretty well. . .

If disputes are indeed concentrated on the larger sites, and there are many reasons for this,[16] what is the nature of the relationship between large sites and the concentration of labour conflicts in a small number of companies? It is simply this: there are only about one hundred companies in New South Wales capable of successfully tendering for, and executing, construction projects valued at one million or more dollars. These companies are responsible for the large sites, hence the concentration of disputes in a small number of companies.

The final general dimension of industrial action concerns the issues which precipitate conflict. Their range is quite limited, tending to centre around wages, conditions, and benefits, managerial behaviour (rather than broad management policy issues), the procedural rules associated with the accommodation system, and union principles.

Wages and conditions tend to dominate not only because this is the traditional rationale for trade union activity, it is also strongly reinforced by the mode of production and the accommodation structure. Job insecurity, the possibility of a fatal accident, the knowledge that the transition to middle age may mean fewer job opportunities, the actual availability of work, and site conditions – including expectations of management – all these factors help to focus discontent around wages and, to a lesser degree, conditions and benefits. Equally potent are the effects of inter-occupational earnings relativities, reinforced in Australia by the predominance of occupational unions. The publicity given to key movements in awards, which frequently cover particular industries or sectors, intensifies coercive wage comparisons. The decline in real wages over recent years is also likely to have led to a keen sensitivity to pay issues. Finally, changes in wages and conditions are the currency most acceptable to employers and tribunals in contrast to control issues, which are generally outside the latter's formal jurisdiction.

Nonetheless, disputes concerning managerial behaviour are relatively frequent and are typically handled by conciliation and compromise. Such issues have their source in the conjunction of a mode of production characterised by instability and uncertainty and an accommodation structure whose procedural rules substantially uphold managerial prerogatives. Instability and uncertainty arise out of the competing requirements of capital and labour. Management, constrained by product market forces, is compelled to maximise efficiency, which includes not only satisfying numerous professional groups, but also using labour as productively as possible. This means an emphasis on contract as opposed to day labour. By contrast, workers desire some certainty of job availability and income. Not surprisingly, disputes centre on dismissals as workers struggle to retain their jobs or attempt to enforce custom and practice termination rules on management. In addition, within the labour process, there is a tendency for management to concentrate on production and profit, with industrial relations regarded more as a constraint than a legitimate policy-making area. This undoubtedly reflects management's values and priorities, but it encourages low trust and inferior communications; these factors frequently underly industrial disputes. Evidence for such attitudes is found in the data on job delegate problems referred to earlier (p.40). The tendency for management and union official responses to the interview statement: 'with the competition and the complexities of production in this industry, management sometimes overlook industrial relation matters, which in turn leads to industrial disputes'. Eighty-one per cent of managers and 97 per cent of union officials agreed with this proposition.

The relative neglect of industrial relations by management cannot be divorced from the prevailing accommodation structure. The Australian system permits joint regulation at workplace level but does not require or even encourage it. This is acknowledged by union officials: 27.6 per cent strongly agreed, and a further 41.4 per cent agreed, with the statement: 'The arbitration system does not encourage union involvement in decision making at workplace level.' Significantly, only 10 per cent of managers reported the existence of a written disputes procedure on their sites, and an even smaller number (5 per cent) said that their company had a comprehensive industrial relations policy. That there is more attention being given to industrial relations by management in the construction industry is perhaps both a reflection of its past neglect and a testimony to the effects of militant trade unionism and the discipline required by a highly competitive product market. It has little to do with the role of the tribunals or governments.

More fundamentally, the accommodation structure itself suffers from a lack of legitimacy despite the acknowledged helpfulness of individual commissioners.[17] The most important trade unions perceive the ground rules as a product of political power, forged by successive governments, which in the main have been hostile to the interests of the labour movement. This political cynicism is evident from the following typical comment:

> The commissioners try and be fair within an unfair system, so they're not really very fair. If they give too much they're pulled into line. The arbitration system is set up as a brake on workers, it's there to prop up the employers' system. It is undemocratic and anti-working class.

Additional evidence of dissatisfaction with the procedural rules governing the accommodation structure is drawn from interview data: 38 per cent of union officials strongly agreed and a further 45 per cent agreed with the statement: 'The legalism and complexity of the arbitration system make union affairs unnecessarily complicated and time consuming'. Preference was given to concluding agreements without the involvement of commissioners: 17.2 per cent and 79.3 per cent of union official respondents strongly agreed and agreed respectively with the statement: 'Employers and unions should settle their claims without recourse to commissioners'. This should not be taken to imply a commitment to a collective bargaining system, but rather a desire to resolve problems without 'outside interference'. There are advantages conferred by awards, which the unions are reluctant to forgo. This is discussed briefly in a later section.

Our general impression of union officials' attitudes to the accommodation structure is that, despite its essentially political and non-consensual ground rules, it was regarded as a fact of life. There were benefits to be gained from pragmatic manipulation of its formal and informal procedures. This included the use of industrial action which was widely believed to influence tribunal decisions. Thus, 48.3 per cent of union officials strongly agreed, and a further 37.9 per cent agreed, with the statement: 'Commissioners only give the worker something if there is pressure to do so'.[18] When asked 'what sort of pressure do you think is most effective', 58.6 per cent referred to strike action and 35 per cent mentioned attendance by workers at tribunal hearings. Black bans were preferred by slightly less than 7 per cent of officials. These data, together with the foregoing argument, suggest that there is likely to be a relatively high proportion of disputes associated with the processes of conciliation and arbitration. This is demonstrated by our data on issues presented in the previous section (Table 2.5, p.33).

It would be unwarranted not to mention the impact of national level wage determination on the distribution of conflict issues. Although wages are the main currency of the system, we drew attention earlier to the ameliorative effect of wage indexation on the frequency of disputes. If that argument is correct, the proportion of wage issues in the total dispute profile should be lower since the commencement of National Wage Indexation. The contention can be assessed with the help of Table 2.11 which, in the absence of New South Wales data, is based on Australia-wide figures.

It is quite clear that wage issues are a substantially smaller proportion of total dispute issues in the period 1976–78. It will be recalled that wage indexation effectively commenced in April 1975. Allowing for a reaction lag of a few months, the data lend support to the view that indexation has affected the distribution of issues precipitating industrial disputes. Although there are no hard data at hand, we also believe that indexation has altered the *types* of issues associated with wage claims. Site allowances have tended to replace over-award claims, these being less difficult to justify in terms of the indexation guidelines.[19]

The final set of issues, those concerning union principles, reflect both unity and cleavage within the union movement. Solidarity issues typically involve unity between workers of different unions. This seems to be

TABLE 2.11

Percentage of disputes involving wage issues in the construction industry,
Australia, 1973-78

	1973	1974	1975	1976	1977	1978
Wage issues as a percentage of total issues	44.2	48.6	39.5	21.2	26.0	27.0
Number of disputes	276	350	309	302	258	178

Source: ABS, *Industrial Disputes*, Cat. no. 6322.0.

evoked by contravention of a strongly held custom and practice rule or infringement of a union principle. An example from the Weekly Reports reads: 'Following the retrenchment of three plasterers . . . the employer was requested to abide by the seniority rule . . . This was rejected by the employer . . . [subsequently]. A meeting of all building workers on site was held. . . ' A further illustration, this time concerning refusals to join a union, and hence 'freeloading' was summarised thus: 'The South Coast Trades and Labor Council placed bans on the supply of pipes and other material to the company after its twelve employees were approached by AWU delegates and refused to become members.'

The comparatively small number of demarcation issues is partly an artefact of the data collection procedures: disputes of this kind are often associated with bans of limited scope, so that, because of their negligible effect on production, there is a tendency for these to be under-reported. But possibly the most important factor contributing to the relatively small number of these disputes, at least by American standards (see Lipsky and Farber, 1976: 389; Foster, 1978: 10–11), is the structure, power, and philosophy of the trade unions.

The BWIU is the predominant tradesmen's union, its leaders and those of the other craft unions believe in principled negotiation and conciliation of inter-union disputes, preferably through the medium of the Building Trades Group. This means that demarcation disputes are likely to be fewer than where the unions are comparatively strong and particularly craft-conscious, as appears to be the case in the United States.[20] Of the demarcation conflicts that do occur, the major axis of cleavage is between the unskilled BLF and the various tradesmen's unions. This is to be expected given the trend towards specialisation and routinisation of what was previously a comprehensive set of skilled tasks.[21]

Our interpretation of the general characteristics of industrial action is now complete. Emphasis has been placed on the mode of production and the accommodation structure as underlying factors that explain the broad features of disputes in this industry. The more detailed patterns of industrial action are considered in the next section.

Industrial Action Patterns: The Dialectics of Union Structures and Strategies

Although use is made of the same basic concepts as in the preceding discussion, Figure 2.1 is provided as a means of aiding the exposition and clarifying the nature of our theory.

FIGURE 2.1
Schematic representation of industrial action model

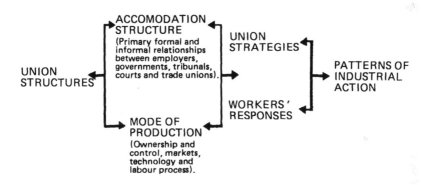

We suggest that the number and character of trade unions in the industry (union structure) represents the product of past interaction between the mode of production and the accommodation structure. This is the point of departure. In order to comprehend the current pattern of industrial action, close attention must be paid to the interplay between present union structures, the mode of production, and the accommodation structure. In particular, the dynamic relationships between market and labour processes on the one hand and the industrial rule-making and enforcement institutions on the other, set the parameters or structural context in which union leaders and workers dialectically develop their strategies, tactics and responses. This changing milieu is both facilitating and constraining: certain strategic options are more realisable than others. Some goals or strategies may be attainable in the short term while others may be 'off the agenda' for the forseeable future. Industrial action is viewed here as a product of the interplay between rank and file attitudes (including the responses evoked by their position in the mode of production) and the strategic actions and policies of union leaders.

If this framework is to prove useful, it should help to explain the five patterns of industrial action by reference to variations in union strategy. These would be influenced by the differing structural contexts of union leaders and members. The analysis will proceed by discussing each of the five patterns in turn.

The Labourers' Pattern: Militant Independence

Frequent single union, workplace instigated, site specific struggles (the autonomous type) and domestic actions are common to both the BLF and AWU. But, as stated earlier, the BLF also engages in single union campaigns and restricted campaign disputes. Since there are significant differences between the organisational processes of these unions, it will be necessary to deal with each in turn, beginning with the BLF.

Following severe intra-union conflict in 1974–75, the Federal Secretary of the BLF appointed several officials to the New South Wales branch. These officers were subsequently replaced by elected personnel who are supporters of the Federal Secretary. The new officials were expected to build and consolidate the union's position in New South Wales; a process made exceptionally difficult by the near bankruptcy of the branch and a massive loss of membership. In addition, the leaders believed they faced membership competition from other unskilled workers' unions, chiefly the AWU, but also the Ironworkers who were attempting to organise unskilled metal workers on construction sites. At the same time, labourers and tradesmen disagreed on several aspects of work demarcation. In particular, the BLF officials feared the growing power of the BWIU, whose proposed amalgamation with the AWU (which subsequently failed) would have brought that union into direct competition with the BLF. In response to its isolation, the BLF adopted a strategy of militant independence. This was encouraged by the Federal Secretary whose personal political position in the higher circles of the labour movement would have been endangered if the New South Wales branch were dominated by the BWIU.

The following extract gives some idea of the BLF leadership's sentiments:

> We stopped other labourers' unions such as the AWU and Ironworkers from taking over the BLF work and reducing BLF's wages. We have won back other work lost by previous BLF leaderships. We have particularly stopped the take-over attempts by the BWIU, BL's want their own union. (BLF, 1972: 2)

The strategy of militant independence is directed towards resolving what is essentially a structural conflict fostered by changes in the mode of production. The de-skilling of craft work and the consequent demise of craft unionism has encouraged greater unity amongst the tradesmen's unions. This has stimulated the BWIU's interest in creating an industry-wide union. The BLF, on the other hand, appears intent on using the decline in skilled work as a pretext for expanding its membership. This structural conflict is exacerbated by the issue of earnings differentials. A BWIU official explained:

> The margin for skill has definitely declined since 1968 . . . you hear a lot of blokes say it's not worth it — there's nothing in it, might as well be a bloody labourer, you don't have to buy and look after tools. The ACTU recommendation was for labourers' to be 85 per cent of tradesman's rates. But labourers' are now about 92 per cent.

With conflict over job territory and pay differentials, it is unlikely that the unskilled and skilled workers' unions can co-operate effectively. This is made more improbable by ideological differences.

The BLF's ideological stance is directly counter to that of the BWIU. Rather than being a separate factor dividing the unions, we would argue that these are, in the main, manifestations of conflicting organisational interests. The leadership of the BLF is associated with the Communist Party of Australia (Marxist–Leninist), the party most sympathetic to Chinese interests. We have been unable to discover the implications of this affiliation for the conduct of trade unionism except in terms of opposition to the BWIU. Briefly, support for China implies an anti-Soviet position. Since the BWIU is sympathetic to the USSR it follows that the BLF is able to maintain its distance from, and criticise, the BWIU in political and industrial terms. However, the BLF leadership is not adverse to unity at the workplace; for example: 'for those who say "unity with the tradesmen" we say "unity with the rank and file tradesmen but not with their so-called leaders." ' (BLF Journal no.3, 1979) The BLF officials are thus opposed to co-operation with BWIU officers on the grounds that their autonomy might be undermined.

A left wing political position implies a preparedness to adopt militant tactics, but, if our argument is correct, militancy should be explicable largely in terms of the mode of production and accommodation structure. This is exactly what our data indicate. To begin with, the BLF organises workers in the most strategically powerful positions on building sites:

> The BLF covers the various non-tradesmen group of workers, including such key jobs as demolition work, crane work, through the dogmen, riggers, scaffolders, hoist drivers, etc. The production on most

major construction projects could be stopped almost in an instant by the action of very few key members of the BLF. (Socialist Party of Australia 1977: 8)

The BLF leaders make use of these key groups. According to the State Secretary: 'We have avoided long and costly strikes. We have been successful with taking industrial action, based on the principle of on-the-job tactics. This means causing most harm to the boss, least harm to ourselves.' Examples from our interviews include 'banning overtime when the company is in a hurry to finish the job, holding a meeting prior to a big concrete pour, and refusing to do certain work'. Strategic power does not by itself encourage frequent use of industrial action. There are two further factors involved in our explanation. These focus on the *effects* of the mode of production and accommodation structure on union organisations.

In interviews with management representatives, it was frequently asserted that BLF full-time officials had a very high turnover rate. This, we would argue, was associated with the abilities of the persons attracted to the organiser's role. With little detailed experience of the award system and union politics, and few negotiating skills, organisers quickly became disenchanted with their job. This in turn encouraged conflicts between officials, which accentuated their dissatisfaction. These processes led to a high union official turnover rate which made it difficult for management to negotiate effectively with the BLF. This is clearly illustrated in the following extracts from our interviews: 'We have a continual problem of new organisers who are inexperienced in demarcation and handling of disputes.' Another manager expressed this view rather more bluntly: 'Quite frankly their (BLF) organisers are thick — they see things in black and white terms. Also, they keep changing.'

The alternative to bargaining is direct action; which undoubtedly achieved short term gains given the strategic power of the BLF members.

In other words, the high frequency of autonomous struggles waged by the BLF has to be understood in the context of the independent strategy of the union, the strategic power of the membership, and the instability of branch union organisation; all these aspects are related to the mode of production. But what of the single union restricted campaign and campaign actions in which the BLF has engaged? These must be seen in relation to the accommodation structure. Faced with campaign type actions encouraged by the BWIU, the BLF leaders have basically two options: to join the other tradesmen's unions in a struggle that may increase relativities between the two major awards, or to independently conduct their own struggle over a wide front. The BLF has tended to prefer the latter strategy, which is compatible with their wish to promote their organisational interests on an independent basis. This is made possible by the existence of separate awards for labourers and tradesmen.

The greater propensity of BLF members to engage in single union restricted campaign and campaign actions in comparison with their AWU counterparts lies in the different relationships between the union organisations and the accommodation structure. Although both unions have separate awards, the BLF's jurisdiction is largely confined to the construction industry, excluding the civil engineering sub-sector. By contrast, the AWU is Australia's second largest union and has coverage of a comparatively small number of unskilled workers who work in the civil engineering sub-sector of the industry. BLF full-time officials, for reasons referred to above, are relatively unrestrained in their instigation of industrial action. Regular visits to large sites occasionally lead to restricted campaign struggles, while campaigns are from time to time planned and directed by the State branch executive, subject of course to the consent, through mass meetings, of the rank and file. These campaigns have become more common as key members of the branch leadership have consolidated their positions in the union.

The AWU suffers from the chronic problem of most large general unions: ensuring that the small specialised sections of the membership are properly serviced. This union has been facing the additional burden of living with the consequences of a major intra-union conflict which led to the establishment of a breakaway organisation in 1977. Not unexpectedly, our on-site observation indicates that AWU members in the construction industry tend to be poorly serviced by their full-time officials. Left to themselves for the most part, these workers tend to engage in single union, single site disputes instigated by influential members or job delegates (autonomous type). Restricted campaign and campaign actions are rare owing to the organisational weakness of the external union.

We have noted that domestic struggles are the second most common type of action engaged in by BLF and AWU members. These reflect work or site-specific conflicts between multi-union work groups or their representatives (site committees) and management. The kind of issues that occasion these disputes include dismissals, site conditions, over-award wages, the use of non-union labour, and other matters of union principle. Members of both unions tend to take action with their BWIU workmates despite the antagonism between the leaders of that union and the BLF.

The BWIU Pattern: United Front

This union's profile is characterised by relatively frequent multi-union campaigns and domestic struggles. BWIU members are also involved in some autonomous actions. The present organisation was born of an amalgamation between the carpenters' and the bricklayers' unions in 1942. Subsequently a merger occurred between several smaller craft unions so that by 1978 the New South Wales branch embraced not only carpenters and joiners (70 per cent), but also bridge and wharf carpenters (3 per cent), bricklayers (22 per cent) and slaters and tile-layers (2.5 per cent). As noted earlier, the Plasterers and Stonemasons are closely associated with the BWIU. Thus, the largest union in the construction industry has a successful record of horizontal expansion. Not surprisingly, its leaders espouse a commitment to industrial unionism which is also associated with a wider political view. The following extract from the State Executive's Report to the 1979 Biennial State Conference also captures the defensive mood of the union:

> With the rapidly changing technology taking place in all industries, including our own, the need to give effect to ACTU policy of industrial unionism holds ever increasing importance ... But of equal or much more importance would be the strengthening of working class organisations and its (sic) ability to successfully fight for working class solutions to the vast changes taking place in our society. The need for positive and constructive discussions and actions to effect amalgamations of unions in the one industry is the only alternative to attempts by some unions to overcome their shrinking membership as a result of technological changes by poaching off areas of other unions.

The way in which the BWIU leaders have persistently put their philosophy of trade union unity into practice can best be seen in relation to the Building Trades Group (BTG). Through this medium, the BWIU has kept other unions informed of its plans, encouraged resolution of inter-union problems, fostered a spirit of community amongst the principal building unions and, most importantly, sought to involve other unions in joint actions and negotiations with employers and the State Government. In short, the very considerable authority the BTG has is largely the consequence of the BWIU's policies although the integrative role played by the Secretary of the Group should not be underestimated.

Attempts by the BWIU to win concessions through unified industrial struggle are exemplified in the leaders' preference for the campaign type of action. In contrast to domestic struggles, which have nevertheless the advantage of unifying the rank and file, campaigns are characterised by organisation and direction tied to strategies carefully worked out in the light of prevailing circumstances. Unlike domestic actions, campaigns unite union leaders and workers in different unions over a wide front. This has the advantage of expressing in symbolic and practical terms some degree of working class unity. But, more importantly from the unions' stand-point, it is one of the limited ways in which trade unions can influence governments.

The size of the BWIU, and hence its importance in the rule-making process (both with respect to the major tradesmen's awards and relevant statutes), means that it is well placed to encourage this type of action. Moreover, the customary practice of 'flow-ons' allows it to concentrate attention on improving this key award and then transmitting these gains to other awards for which it is responsible. It is mainly the institutionalisation of the flow-on process that encourages union preference for awards and hence by implication, inhibits the spread of unregistered collective agreements.[22] As one BWIU official observed:

> This initially affects our tactics because if we develop a policy of seeking industrial agreements with the MBA [Master Builders' Association of New South Wales] rather than seeking to get gains into the award itself, we destroy the flow process, which operates to our advantage, because we are able to use the power base in the construction industry to flow it through.

This point is particularly relevant to occupational unions, who, like the BWIU, have small pockets of members covered by different awards to which the union is usually a minority party.

Despite a preference for campaign actions, the majority of disputes in which BWIU members are involved are of the domestic type. This indicates the influence of the mode of production. With the exception of larger sites, tradesmen covered by the BWIU are difficult to organise. This is largely because of the frequency of job change and the growth of sub-contracting. It is common knowledge that many tradesmen prefer to be paid 'money in the hand' (thereby often evading tax) rather than accepting employment on the basis of the award.[23] Campaigns, therefore, require careful consideration if the rank and file are to be successfully mobilised in a time of recession. By contrast, domestic struggles, based on problems experienced in common with members of other unions (especially labourers), are easier to undertake. These are not discouraged by BWIU officials who tend to believe that workers benefit from the experience of organising their own disputes, especially where these serve to unify members of different unions. But, for the most part, domestic actions occur irrespective of official union attitudes simply because there are insufficient organisers available to resolve problems that occur on the large number of sites scattered over a great area.

To conclude our argument in relation to the BWIU, despite the relative size of this union, it is facing the prospect of a long term decline in membership because of changes in the mode of production. If this is to be reversed, increasing unionisation of contract workers[24] and further horizontal expansion is necessary. The building of unity through militant action, especially in multi-union campaigns and, to a lesser extent, domestic struggles, serves as one of several bases for future amalgamation. By improving the rewards and reducing the deprivations of its members the BWIU also hopes to attract new members.

The Craft Pattern: Moderate Dependence

The five craft unions rarely engage in industrial struggle, and when they do, it is generally only in a multi-union campaign action. The craft unions, as noted earlier (p.30), are very small. With the exception of the Plumbers they also possess little bargaining power. This is evident from a cursory examination of their organisational resources and lack of control over the labour supply.

Although information on union assets and liabilities is not readily available, the most recent data from official sources (Report of the Industrial Registrar under the Trade Union Act, 1881, for 1976, no.312) permit appropriate comparisons to be made between unions on the basis of current revenue and expenditure. This information is summarised in Table 2.12.

TABLE 2.12

Excess of revenue over expenditure per union member: BWIU and Craft Unions, New South Wales 1976

Union	BWIU	ASC&J	Painters	Plasterers	Plumbers	Stonemasons
Dollars	45.9	6.5	6.4	26.1	18.1	32.0

Source: Calculated from Trade Unions — Members receipts, Expenditure and Funds 1976, p.6, *Report of the Industrial Registrar*, 1976.

The figures for the Plasterers and Stonemasons do not accurately portray the financial position of these unions, because they use BWIU administrative resources that attract only a nominal charge. Bearing this in mind, it is reasonable to conclude that the craft unions are, in financial terms, comparatively weak. In organisation their position is no better, again with the exception of the Plumbers, who have recently obtained statutory registration provisions.[25] The other principal crafts unions have suffered from the de-skilling effects of technological change, so that today apprenticeship is not the sole, or even the most common, requirement to engage in tradesmen's work. The unions will join up practically any person who is 'on the tools'. Even this is difficult, given the increasing trend towards sub-contracting.

The craft unions have essentially three choices open to them: the first is to continue to try to preserve their craft status and independence in the face of overwhelming odds; the second is to increase co-operation with other craft unions and, more especially, with the relatively large BWIU; the third alternative, which has generally been preceded by the second, is that of amalgamation, again with the BWIU. Only the Plumbers have successfully maintained their independence and craft status.

Although this union has sufficient power and resources to engage in industrial struggle, there are four reasons why such action has been infrequent. In the first place, the market position of plumbers, both over the long and short run, has been much more favourable than other building trades. Secondly, licensing of plumbers has fostered an easy transition from worker to sub-contractor. In this connection a union official has commented that:

> a third of the membership would have had a go on their own – and we'd encourage them to – but they don't stay there, they come back into the industry because they don't like the hassle of going around pricing work, and they might find the competition a bit stiff.

The two facts of a favourable market situation and opportunities for working independently mean that the plumbers' specific mode of production is not conducive to the development of union militancy. This is reinforced by the notion of margin for skill institutionalised in the accommodation process. Plumbers are therefore likely to maintain their wage relativity especially since skill requirements, in contrast to other unions, have increased with technological change. Registration is an institutionalised acknowledgement of this claim. Finally, the branch leadership has been conservative, preferring to tread along well established paths rather than to develop new goals and strategies. Nevertheless, faced with intra-union faction problems and demarcation disputes with the BLF, the Plumbers have sought a closer liaison with other unions in the BTG.

The remaining craft unions, with little power at their disposal, have had the option of closer association with the other unions, especially the BWIU, or amalgamation. The ASC&J has strongly resisted amalgamation and has confined co-operation with the BWIU and the BTG to a minimum. This stems mainly from the leadership's ideological hostility to the left wing BWIU, coupled with a fear of losing their organisational identity. The Painters, on the other hand, have sought close co-operation with other craft unions and the BWIU. This union attempted to amalgamate with the BWIU in 1967. A plebiscite failed to carry a majority in Victoria and Tasmania so that the merger did not take place (Harrowfield, 1978). Good relations between the Painters and the BWIU have, nonetheless, persisted. Finally, there are plans for the Plasterers and Stonemasons to conclude arrangements for amalgamation with the BWIU in 1980.

This short digression into craft union relationships has been necessary, for it illustrates the narrow set of options available to these unions. Partly as a consequence of their structural position (of weakness) and partly owing to the skill and effectiveness of the BWIU leadership, the craft unions have been drawn into a symbiotic relationship with that union. In exchange for support against job territory incursions by the BLF and provision of administrative resources, the craft unions have, in association with the BWIU and under the umbrella of the BTG, engaged in campaign struggles. Underlying these political processes is a history of craft union co-operation in relation to common awards and a shared interest in improving the National Building Trades Construction Award.

In sum, the craft unions are rarely involved in industrial action, this being mainly a result of their organisational precariousness. The mode of production has encouraged them to seek greater co-operation with the BWIU which, as we demonstrated earlier, engages in campaign type struggles. The craft unions are associated with these actions on account of their relationship to the accommodation structure.

The General Peripheral Pattern: Mixed Militancy

Like the BWIU, members of the two peripheral unions that organise skilled and semi-skilled workers (the AMWSU, the Amalgamated Metal Workers and Shipwrights' Union, and FEDFA, the Federated Engine Drivers and Firemen's Association of Australasia) participate in domestic, autonomous, and multi-union campaign actions. There are two particular reasons for their high involvement in domestic struggles. Like the BLF, these unions organise strategically powerful groups; the AMWSU, for example, covers boilermakers and welders, and crane drivers are members of the FEDFA. But, unlike the BLF, these unions do not have many members on construction sites, so they seek solidarity with members of other unions. More commonly they are called upon to take a lead in action on behalf of their workmates.

The second reason for participation in domestic disputes is that the union organisers, like the BWIU officials, are unable to visit sites as the need arises and particularly when major site-level disagreements occur. In any case they tend to regard small scale conflict as a fact of life. Consistent with the ideology held by most officials in these two unions, there is a preference for 'unity on the job' when disputes do take place. This is underpinned by a traditional trade union principle as one union official explained: 'We support united action . . . the weak can be assisted by the strong. We don't believe unions should act in isolation.' Given this predisposition, why are the activities of these unions not directed towards a greater number of multi-union campaign struggles?

The point worth emphasising here is that members of these unions do participate in many campaigns, though these constitute only a small proportion of the total number of disputes in which these unions are involved. Such campaigns are most common in the fixed establishments within the public sector, where members of these unions work alongside carpenters and are covered by common awards.[26] On construction sites, however, AMWSU and FEDFA members are governed by separate awards.[27] Their peripheral status means that these workers are rarely expected to participate in campaigns involving the other principal construction unions.

One quarter of disputes involving the AMWSU and FEDFA are of the autonomous type. The key to understanding this is the place of certain members of these unions in the division of labour. Welders and boiler-makers will serve as examples.

These workers often work in small gangs isolated socially, and often geographically (for example on pipe lines), from their fellows. They tend to possess considerable strategic power since production or maintenance can be halted in a short space of time. Their isolation, monopoly of skills, group cohesion, and small numbers generally facilitate speedy dispute settlements on terms eventually acceptable to management and workers. In short, the power of these occupational groups encourages single union, workplace instigated, site-specific actions. These we term autonomous disputes.

The general peripheral pattern may now be summarised. Members of AMWSU and FEDFA enjoy a favourable bargaining position. The way in which this power is translated into action is in part shaped by their position in the labour process and partly by the peripheral nature of these unions' relationships to the dominant accommodation structure. Domestic struggles are facilitated by grievances shared with members of other unions and the role played by union organisers. Multi-union campaign actions occur, especially where members of these unions are parties to common awards with the principal construction unions. By contrast, autonomous disputes are more common where occupational groups are relatively isolated and socially cohesive.

The Peripheral Craft Pattern: Moderate Independence

In terms of its key organisational characteristics the ETU (Electrical Trades Union of Australia) resembles the Plumbers: by Australian craft union standards both are relatively large, possess some control over the labour supply, and are managed in New South Wales by moderate union leaders. These officials are frequently in conflict with their federal executives which are dominated by left-wing officers. The ETU differs significantly from the Plumbers in that most of its members are not associated with the construction industry.

For similar reasons to those given in the discussion of the Plumbers (pp.57) the ETU's dispute pattern resembles that of the craft unions: both groups rarely engage in industrial action. However, Table 2.8 shows that electricians tend to engage in a smaller proportion of multi-union campaigns but a greater relative number of domestic actions. Why should this be so?

The ETU is party to awards in common with construction unions only in the fixed establishments located in the public sector.[28] The smaller proportion of multi-union campaigns is largely attributable to this. It reflects the peripheral relationship between the union and the construction industry. The tendency towards greater relative participation in domestic struggles is closely associated with the mode of production, particularly the division of labour. Electricians work alongside other workers on construction sites. Although inclined to maintain their independence from other occupational groups, these workers are subject to the same general site conditions and supervision as members of other unions. In addition, ETU job delegates are represented on some site committees. Members of the ETU are, therefore, involved in disputes on issues affecting most or all workers on any particular site, or those requiring solidarity with members of other unions. Their relatively greater involvement in these types of disputes is associated with their superior strategic power in comparison with most other craft unions. The craft characteristics of the ETU, the relationship that this union has to the prevailing accommodation structure, and the position of the members in the division of labour are the principal reasons for the dispute pattern described earlier.

Conclusions

This chapter has focused on the relationships between union structure, the mode of production, and the accommodation system as the major influences on both the general features and particular organisational attributes of industrial action in the construction industry. The theoretical and research implications of our study are included in the general discussion of these issues in the final chapter of this book (pp.159). Here we restrict ourselves to an assessment of future developments in industrial conflict in the construction industry.

There appear to be forces both facilitating and containing collective action. Certainly, keen market competition, the present tendering system, persistent job insecurity, the de-skilling of work, and the growth of sub-contracting are conducive to labour conflict. On the other hand these factors associated with the mode of production are being regulated to a greater extent than hitherto as a result of changes affecting the accommodation structure. As mentioned earlier, there has been a trend towards greater unity, centralisation, and joint regulation over the past few years. Significantly, for the first time a disputes procedure has been negotiated and included in the most recent Builders' Labourers' award (1979). The greater attention management is now paying to industrial relations is especially important. Worker participation schemes have attracted substantial managerial interest, and it is quite possible that the eighties will witness greater experimentation in, and formalisation of, site-level relations.

We would hazard a guess that at least as long as the recession persists there will be a moderate level of disputes. The trend towards unity and centralisation on both sides of industry point towards the emergence of national, as opposed to State-wide, multi-union campaigns. But mobilisation problems are likely to restrict the frequency of such activity. Meanwhile, site-specific disputes will continue, given the existing mode of production. This scenario may, however, be invalidated by two institutional changes: further inter-union or intra-union conflict and attempts by a national government to ensure trade union acquiesence in what is essentially a policy of statist corporatism (Crouch, 1977: 33–44). Both are possibilities that would inflict great damage on the delicate bargaining relationships that are beginning to develop in this most fascinating industry.

NOTES

1. Newspaper headlines referring to the construction industry in the *Sydney Morning Herald*, 15th July 1978 p.3 and p.21 and *The Australian*, 28th June, 1978.
2. See Haskall, 1977 and Roddewig, 1978.
3. See P. Thomas, 1973 and Socialist Party of Australia, 1977.
4. The Weekly Reports of Industrial Disputes are compiled by officers of the Department of Employment and Industrial Relations. Employers and trade unions are not legally obliged to provide information to the Department (reconstituted as the Department of Industrial Relations in December 1978). ABS dispute data is comparable with that supplied by the Department; indeed, the Weekly Reports are one of the major sources on which the Bureau relies in order to dispatch their dispute questionnaires. Employers and unions are legally required to complete these forms which remain confidential and are therefore unavailable for research purposes.
5. The construction industry is variously defined by the parties in the industry. This definition excludes the manufacture of parts and suppliers of building materials. Thus, disputes in ancillary establishments such as quarries, brickworks, and concrete plants are excluded.
6. A significant recent example of these trends was the establishment in 1974 of the National Industrial Executive, an umbrella organisation for the MBFA (Master Builders' Federation of Australia) and AFCC (Australian Federation of Construction Contractors). This body has been given authority to formulate policies, develop

strategy, and organise implementation in national industrial relations matters. Also of note is the recent formation of the Construction Industry Research Committee sponsored jointly by the MBFA and the AFCC. This committee has issued two reports, one concerning site-level relationships and another dealing with the effectiveness of the present structure of employer associations in the construction industry.

7. Labor councils are inter-union bodies established on a regional basis. They are branches of the ACTU.

8. 'Flow-ons' have been curtailed by the guidelines of the AC&AC, which restrict all wage increases other than those deriving from national indexation decisions to those meeting one or more of the criteria specified in the guidelines. See Plowman, 1979.

9. The year 1975 marked the turning point in the building boom and in the number of disputes. Consequently, we have examined the period following this, that is, 1976-78, the most recent period for which data is available.

10. Using accident data provided by the Workers' Compensation Commission of New South Wales, it was estimated that of nineteen industry categories, construction ranked among the four highest in 1976 and 1977.

11. Personal communications from the Builders' Licensing Board and New South Wales Corporate Affairs Commission, 1978.

12. Managers generally mentioned two types of absenteeism: firstly, the common phenomenon of 'taking sickies', that is using up the amount of sick leave specified in the award; secondly, that form of absenteeism typified by the employee who works only three or four days per week to earn sufficient to finance his increased leisure time.

13. These job delegates from several principal construction unions completed a questionnaire in 1978. We have continued to administer these questionnaires in 1979 and 1980. It should be noted that job delegates are not regarded as 'stirrers' by the great majority of management interviewees, rather they are seen having similar attitudes to rank and file construction workers.

14. A 'paid rate award' stipulates total earnings. In determining the exact level, the Commission combined the previous award minimum with the amount bargained at site level to yield a maximum rate of pay. The subsequent indexation based on the 'paid rate' put the wages of building workers far ahead of metal tradesmen, the traditional wage leaders.

15. These include accident pay (full pay when off work on a compensatable injury), a long service leave scheme, a safety code, and ten days paid sick leave per year.

16. These are similar factors to those referred to in the general discussion included in .Chapter 6 (pp.150). In addition, the duration of larger projects generally means that specific groups of workers have longer periods of employment. This, together with the larger number of men involved, facilitates the development of shop steward organisation.

17. It should be emphasised that 17 per cent and 72 per cent of the union officials interviewed strongly agreed and agreed respectively with the statement 'Commissioners are usually helpful because they try and get the parties to agree rather than make a decision for them'.

18. Commissioners disagree with this assessment. All Commissioners interviewed stressed that industrial action had no influence on the content of their decisions.

19. See Australian Conciliation and Arbitration Commission, April 1975, September 1978.

20. Notes on a discussion between BWIU officials and Professor George Strauss, 24th October, 1979.

21. For example, much formwork is regarded as 'rough' carpentry. The introduction of metal parts and fabrication off-site has lessened the amount of skilled work on-site. Furthermore, power tools have reduced the degree of skill necessary to undertake many tasks.

22. One union official indicated that employer associations often favour an award structure for organisational reasons. 'Awards suit the employers' associations because if we only have an agreement with them [the unions] then the scope is restricted to members of organisations who are parties to the agreement and that is an incentive for members to avoid the agreement and resign from the association.'

23. Advantages to employers include reduced overhead costs, no workers' compensation or insurance premiums, and no long service leave payments.

24. The BTG are campaigning vigorously for contract prices in the housing sub-sector to be fixed by law. Employers believe this to be part of an attempt to unionise this section of the industry. See Commission of Inquiry into the Nature and Terms of Employment in the New South Wales Housing Industry, 1979–80. The report and recommendations of the Commissioner are to be presented in late March 1980.

25. The Plumbers and Gasfitters Registration Act 1979 was gazetted in January 1980; it requires all plumbers to be registered. For some time plumbers have had to be licenced and as a result of this, a high proportion of plumbers have been apprenticed in comparison with the other construction trades.

26. For example, Crown Employees (Skilled Trades) Award and Public Hospitals Skilled Tradesmen (State) (Interim) Award.

27. The award covering FEDFA members is the Plant Operators on Construction State Award. Metal workers are employed under various Federal and State metal industry awards.

28. An example of this is the award covering maintenance tradesmen in the public hospitals in New South Wales. In general, electricians working on construction sites are employed under the terms of either the Electricians State Award or the Metal Industry Award. The MTIA (Metal Trades Industries Association) has recently been negotiating for a construction appendix to the Metal Industry Award.

CHAPTER THREE

Sectionalism, Solidarity and Action in Shipbuilding and Shiprepair*

Victor G. Taylor

Labour history assigns shipbuilding and shiprepair to the leading ranks of conflict-prone industries. Even before the Australian industry became firmly established, with the help of British capital and labour, the Webbs were already lamenting the state of industrial relations in English ship-yards. On Tyneside in the early 1890s they pointed out that:

> Within the space of thirty-five months, there were no fewer than thirty-five weeks in which one or other of the four most important sections of workmen in the staple industry of the district absolutely refused to work. This meant the stoppage of huge establishments, the compulsory idleness of tens of thousands of other artisans and labour-ers, the selling up of households, and the semi-starvation of thousands of families totally unconcerned with the dispute (Webb, 1919: 513).

Some notable struggles have been recorded in the Australian industry. For example, when Judge Beeby of the Conciliation and Arbitration Court de-registered the AEU (Amalgamated Engineering Union) for nine months in 1938, the proximate cause was a protracted work stoppage by workers at two Sydney dockyards over a claim for payment of a ship repair allowance (Sheridan, 1975: 133–5). More recently, in 1974, the Federal Minister for Transport established an Overseas Study Mission to investigate aspects of the shipbuilding industry. This step was taken for a number of reasons, a major one being concern over the relationship

*I wish to thank Duncan Macdonald and other contributors to this volume for their comments on earlier drafts of this chapter. In the concluding stages of preparation Steve Frenkel rescued me from many ambiguities, naiveties and indiscretions. Opinions and shortcomings which remain are my responsibility alone.

between discordant industrial relations and productivity (Report of Australian Shipbuilding Industry Study Mission, 1975: ix). Emphasising this theme in 1976, the Prime Minister offered orders to two major shipbuilding yards provided that, among other things, workers agreed to a wage freeze and a complete moratorium on industrial action (The Fraser Plan, *Newcastle Morning Herald*, 28 August 1976). These developments point to a need for systematic analysis of industrial conflict in the shipbuilding and shiprepair industry (hereafter shipbuilding), especially since simplistic diagnoses predominate. A popular view amongst managers and government officials for example, is that the poor state of industrial relations arises from the plotting of ideologically motivated union militants and continual demarcation disputes. This chapter specifically addresses the issue of industrial action in the period 1975–78, a time of severe recession in the shipbuilding industry. Future prospects seem so bleak that it appears apt to refer to Australian shipbuilding as a declining industry.

The principal sources of dispute data used in the analysis include the Weekly Reports compiled by the Department of Employment and Industrial Relations and records provided by the management of a large commercial shipyard. Some reference is also made to a survey conducted in 1977 among 443 workers from the same yard, as part of a redundancy case study.[1]

The chapter is divided into three parts. The first section describes the main features of the industry; this is followed by an examination of the industrial action profile. Two contrasting patterns are identified, the first and more common type of industrial action is restricted to relatively small collectivities, while the second variant encompasses much larger action units. An explanation of these dispute patterns is provided in section three. The chapter concludes with some brief remarks about the future of industrial relations in the shipbuilding industry.

Key Features of the Shipbuilding and Shiprepair Industry

Shipbuilding derives many of its present practices and customs from a pre-mechanised era. Based on the principle of large-scale unit production (Woodward, 1965: 37), work processes are highly specialised and controlled through a craft method of administration (Stinchcombe, 1959). Many shipbuilding workers are highly skilled and enjoy considerable autonomy, though working conditions can be unpleasant. Tasks associated with design, hull construction, and fitting-out are performed sequentially, so demand for the labour of various occupations is uneven and varies over time for any particular skill group.

The market for new vessels is insufficient to ensure that existing plant and equipment are used at full capacity. Apart from the naval sub-sector, competition is very keen, and much emphasis is placed on meeting completion deadlines. Commercial contracts frequently include financial penalty clauses that reflect high interest and opportunity costs. With small profit margins, liquidity is a major problem for ship constructors, who are especially dependent upon progress payments disbursed according to work completed.

Large commercial shipbuilding has always received a measure of protection from open market forces. For much of the post-war period up to 1976, Australian fleet operators had to obtain ministerial approval if they wished to buy, build, or lease ships from overseas. To cushion the cost disadvantages of owners purchasing Australian built vessels, the Federal Government has paid a subsidy to yards building larger ships.[2]

During the seventies, the growing ability of overseas yards to reduce costs and prices through economies of scale and high capitalisation, led some Australian shipowners to press for a review of protection arrangements for the industry. An inquiry was held by the Industries Assistance Commission at the Government's request in 1976. The findings lent support to the existing policy of successive reductions in subsidy rates and also prompted the removal of most major import restrictions. As a consequence, the industry suffered exposure to severe overseas competition, and there was a dramatic decline in orders. Thus, between 1973 and 1978 the number of larger yards was reduced from six to two, with an associated reduction of 75 per cent in their labour requirements.[3]

Decline has not been uniform throughout the industry. In contrast to commercial shipbuilding, the naval sub-sector has been less drastically affected by overseas competition and world-wide recession.[4] This is largely because the Government is committed, for defence reasons, to the maintenance of a limited shipbuilding and repair capability. At present, one private and two state-owned yards undertake defence work and each of these employs more than 1000 manual workers.[5]

A third sub-sector, which mainly involves shiprepair, consists of about fifty establishments and is highly competitive. Most firms also engage in marine engineering and associated work, and, with few exceptions, employ less than fifty workers. While demand for the services of these enterprises is notoriously unstable, the high opportunity cost of delays in the movement of cargo generates considerable pressures for prompt completion of work. Managers refer to this sub-sector as one dictated by 'time and tide'. It is estimated that overseas competition has reduced the labour force in these firms by 20 per cent in the space of five years (1973–78), with approximately 3500 remaining employed at June 1978.[6]

Taken as a whole, the shipbuilding industry lost about 30 per cent of its workers between 1973 and 1978. By the end of this period there were 12 000 employees in the industry. This represented only 0.2 per cent of the Australian labour force compared with the still marginal figure of 0.3 per cent in 1973.[7]

The composition of the shipbuilding labour force is quite distinctive. Between 50 and 60 per cent of manual workers are skilled tradesmen. Within their ranks is an extremely diverse range of occupations including boilermakers, fitters, sheetmetal workers, electricians, shipwrights, joiners, furniture makers, sailmakers, crane operators, plumbers, coppersmiths, and quite a few more. The remaining semi-skilled and unskilled groups include painters and dockers, ironworker tradesmen's assistants, drivers, storemen, riggers, and labourers. Occupational heterogeneity is a key feature of the industry, but intra-occupational cohesion tends to be high. Some groups, like painters and dockers and shipwrights in certain large centres, display many of the characteristics associated with the notion of an occupational community (Salaman, 1974).

In common with most declining industries, there appears to be a high proportion of older workers in the shipbuilding industry. In one typical large yard more than a half of the manual workers were over forty-five years in contrast to the 'all industry' equivalent figure of 33 per cent (see ABS, *1976 Census*, Catalogue no.2426.0). It is also noteworthy that practically all manual workers are male.

The shipbuilding industry has long been a trade union stronghold. A

TABLE 3.1

Approximate distribution of manual union members in shipbuilding and shiprepair industry, Australia, mid 1976

Union	Occupational coverage	%
AMWSU*	Fitters, boilermakers, sheet metal workers, coppersmiths, shipwrights, etc.	40
FIA	Tradesmen's assistants, labourers	20
FSPDU	Painters and dockers, riggers	15
ETU	Electrical tradesmen	5
ASE	Engineering tradesmen	3
BWIU	Joiners, wood machinists	2
FEDFA	Crane drivers	2
PGEU	Plumbing tradesmen	2
Other unions	Craftsmen, drivers, storemen, etc.	10

*Includes The FSSCA (Federated Shipwrights and Ship Constructors' Association of Australia) which amalgamated with the AMWU to form the AMWSU in November, 1976.

Source: Derived from Industries Assistance Commission (1976), and unpublished naval dockyards labour force data.

de facto closed shop has operated in most medium and large establishments since the turn of the century. Union structure is complex; its origins lie in the traditional, detailed division of labour. Over time trade union boundaries and occupational categories have reinforced one another to a considerable degree. Labour fragmentation remains high, as demonstrated by the fact that there are sixteen union signatories to the Port of Sydney Ship Repairing and Ship Building Agreement,[8] with a further three unions known to have members in local establishments. Furthermore, another eight unions organise non-manual labour in the industry.

The distribution of union members and their occupations is shown in Table 3.1.

Three unions account for 75 per cent of the manual labour force. The conglomerate AMWSU covers about 40 per cent, with the bulk of its membership among skilled metal tradesmen and shipwrights, while the FIA (Federated Ironworkers Association of Australia) and FSPDU (Federated Ship Painters and Dockers' Union of Australia), both of which organise semi-skilled and unskilled workers, are responsible for 20 per cent and 15 per cent respectively. The remaining 25 per cent of manual workers are organised by a host of unions, each with very limited membership. Indeed, with the important exception of the FSPDU, no union of any size has more than 5 per cent of its members in the shipbuilding industry.

Rimmer and Sutcliffe (1979: 16) point out that shipbuilding was one of the first industries in which shop committees emerged. This tradition of union organisation has continued: the larger unions at major yards have operated senior delegate representation systems for many years and, in addition, regularly scheduled formal meetings of joint union organisations, most of which have active executive committees, remain standard practice in both naval and larger commercial yards. Typically, representation on these yard committees is on the basis of occupation, so the AMWSU provides the largest single group, and delegates of this union usually fill the key executive posts. Occupational representation contributes to the large size of these bodies with more than thirty eligible delegates not uncommon.

Management in the industry also displays a number of features relevant to an understanding of industrial action. In commercial establishments, most senior management personnel have had a production background and often hold a professional engineering qualification. The impact of these characteristics on industrial relations is difficult to determine, but in some instances there is evidence of considerable alienation of workers from top management. Thus, 90 per cent of the 443 respondents surveyed in 1977 felt that senior managers were remote from them and only 23 per cent agreed that 'most top management are really concerned for their workers'.

Rapport between senior management and manual workers is made more difficult in the two state-owned naval yards where the general managers are senior naval officers, while industrial relations managers are career public servants. These characteristics seem to foster a unitary frame of reference (see Fox, 1966: 3 and Committee of Enquiry into Industrial Relations in Naval Dockyards, 1975: 72), while the high turnover of industrial relations managers reduces the consistency of decision-making.

Supervisors and foremen in shipbuilding are recruited from the shop floor. Many retain their occupational identities, and even their union membership, and are strongly aware of the many local custom and practice rules that have developed over a long period. Within limits set by budgets, which they help to formulate, considerable decision-making discretion remains; payment of disability rates and establishment of manning levels are two important areas under the control of lower management.

Although the majority of the larger employers prefer to develop their own labour relations practices, most private firms are members of the MTIA. This employer association maintains a committee in New South Wales specifically concerned with shipbuilding industrial relations. It appears that increased overseas competition has provided an incentive for greater co-operation amongst employers, evidenced by the signing in 1976 of the Port of Sydney Ship Repairing and Ship Building Agreement by the MTIA and officials of the New South Wales Labor Council.

In addition to national level wage indexation decisions, the industry is regulated through a two-tiered accommodation structure. Wage rates and other key substantive matters are determined at industry level with the Federal Metal Industry Award occupying a central place. Despite the fact that not all unions are parties to this award, (for example, both the painters and dockers, and shipwrights have their own federal awards), it has nevertheless been the pattern setter. Moreover, movements in the Metal Award are nearly always reflected in conditions applying to shipbuilding workers in Department of Defence naval yards through variations in the relevant public service determination.[9]

Negotiation of the previously mentioned Port of Sydney Agreement, encompassing virtually all the unions, emphasised the special requirements of the industry and, in effect, endorsed the primacy of industry-level accommodation in one of the largest shipbuilding centres. There has also been a strong tendency to minimise negotiations on pay at establishment level; indeed, the Port of Sydney Agreement, with certain qualifications, prohibits wage bargaining between annual negotiations.[10]

The second tier of the accommodation structure, and the most important from the point of view of everyday industrial relations, consists of a myriad of intra-yard informal custom and practice rules, together with a small number of formal plant-wide procedural agreements. The latter are designed to limit industrial action taken in the context of demarcation disputes.

The Shape of Industrial Action

The various dimensions of industrial action can be conveniently discussed under two headings: firstly, the general attributes, which refer to the incidence, form, duration, and issues associated with overt industrial conflict; and secondly, the organisational characteristics, including the scope, union involvement, and leadership aspects of organised militancy.

General Attributes of Industrial Action

Unpublished ABS data covering the period 1973–78 show clearly that shipbuilding has a relatively high incidence of strikes. Over these six years, the industry accounted for 4.3 per cent of all disputes, 2.6 per cent of worker involvement, and 1.5 per cent of total time 'lost'. Recalling that employment has been between 0.2 and 0.3 per cent of the Australian labour force, these data place the industry among the most dispute-prone in the country, although in the later years of the period, notably 1976 and 1977, some signs of moderation are evident. On average, about six strikes per month were recorded by the ABS between 1975 and 1978. This is very similar to the rate indicated in the Weekly Reports.[11]

Although strikes are by far the most commonly reported form of industrial action (72 per cent), it is also evident that other methods are used to exert pressure on management. *Ad hoc* and regular stop-work meetings accounted for 16.3 per cent of the total while overtime and work bans made up the remaining 11.7 per cent of all recorded actions. Worker militancy appears to be confined to the naval and larger commercial yards (85 per cent), but exactly how much this reflects under-reporting by smaller firms is difficult to determine.[12]

The short duration of shipbuilding disputes is clearly implied in the ABS figures presented above; these indicate that the industry's share of dispute frequency is well ahead of its share of time 'lost'. This is confirmed by examination of the frequency distribution of work stoppages reported in the Weekly Reports. These show that 70.6 per cent of stoppages are concluded within two days while only 7 per cent continued for ten days or more.[13] It is noteworthy that bans tend to be applied for longer periods. Of twenty-five bans for which sufficiently detailed information is available, two-thirds were in force for more than ten days.

The issues that precipitate industrial disputes are presented in Table 3.2.

TABLE 3.2

Distribution of industrial disputes by cited issue, shipbuilding and ship repair industry, Australia, 1975-78

Cited issue	Number of disputes %		Working days 'lost' %	
Pay		22.4		27.4
National/district wage claims	4.2		8.8	
Domestic wage claims	8.0		12.6	
Decisions on payment of established disability and special rates etc.	8.8		4.4	
Other	1.4		1.6	
Leave, pensions, compensation		0.3		0.0
Management policy and behaviour		22.4		22.7
Dismissals and discipline	8.8		9.6	
Manning and work allocation	13.6		13.1	
Physical working conditions		7.0		3.9
Trade unionism		34.0		18.7
Intra-union communication	18.6		1.5	
Demarcation	12.9		13.5	
Other	2.5		3.7	
Declining industry prospects		7.3		17.1
Political		3.8		6.4
Other		2.8		3.8
Total		100.0		100.0
Number of disputes, working days 'lost'		286		153 972

Source: Weekly Reports, Department of Employment and Industrial Relations.

Pay and management policy and behaviour each account for about a quarter of total disputes, and a further one-third are associated with trade unionism, chiefly intra-union communications (18.6 per cent) and demarcation (12.9 per cent). Although stoppages over declining industry prospects and political matters taken together only represent 11.1 per cent of total disputes, these account for nearly a quarter (23.5 per cent) of total time 'lost'. Since 89.3 per cent of these stoppages are concluded in less than two days, the evidence indicates that large numbers of workers are involved in action over these issues.

Organisational Features and Patterns of Industrial Action

The term 'work-unit' has been devised in order to distinguish between disputes that are restricted to workers who form a sectional action group and those that demonstrate a wider solidarity. Members of the same work-unit either work together or share a common leisure area (amenities block or shed) that provides opportunities for daily interaction. Table 3.3 categorises disputes according to organisational scope and whether action is restricted to one or more work-units and unions.

TABLE 3.3

Organisational scope of industrial disputes in shipbuilding and ship repair industry, Australia, 1975–78.

Organisational scope	Number of disputes %	%
Intra-yard		76.6
Single work-unit: single union	56.7	
Single work-unit: multi-union	11.2	
Multiple work-unit: single union	1.7	
Multiple work-unit: multi-union	7.0	
Yard-wide and multi-yard		23.4
Single union	6.7	
Multi-union	16.7	
Total		100.0
Number of disputes		286

Source: Weekly Reports, Department of Employment and Industrial Relations.

Over three-quarters of all stoppages (76.6 per cent) are confined to specific yards. The great majority of these are restricted to single work-units whose members are confined to one union (56.7 per cent). Nearly a quarter (23.4 per cent) of labour conflicts involve action units that span one or more establishments and in contrast to the sectional disputes referred to above, these tend to involve several unions acting in concert (16.7 per cent of total disputes).[14]

The participation of unions in work stoppages varies a good deal both in relation to involvement in single union and multi-union activity. This can be seen by inspection of the data included in Table 3.4.

TABLE 3.4

Industrial disputes by union, shipbuilding and ship repair industry, Australia 1975–78

Union	Single union disputes %	Multi-union disputes %	All disputes %
AMWSU	22.5*	72.7	39.9
FIA	2.7	83.8	30.8
FSPDU	31.6	56.6	40.2
ETU	10.2	44.4	22.0
ASE	0.0	48.5	16.8
BWIU	4.8	41.4	17.5
FEDFA	4.3	43.4	17.8
PGEU	3.7	42.4	17.1
FMWU	8.6	36.4	18.2
Other	11.6	n.a.	n.a.
Number of disputes	187	99	286

*This figure includes FSSCA (Shipwrights) disputes prior to amalgamation with the AMWU in 1976. These account for 8.6 per cent of all single union disputes.

Source: Weekly Reports, Department of Employment and Industrial Relations.

Single union disputes are twice as numerous as their multi-union equivalents, and the FSPDU, with less than a fifth of the labour force, is involved in nearly a third (31.6 per cent) of single union conflicts. The AMWSU also shows a relatively high participation rate in these disputes (22.5 per cent), but it will be recalled that 40 per cent of shipyard workers are members of this union. Of note, too, is the low involvement of the FIA in single union actions (2.7 per cent), bearing in mind that this is the second largest union in the industry.

With regard to multi-union disputes, the AMWSU and FIA are most active (72.7 per cent and 83.8 per cent respectively), while the other unions participate in a substantial number, albeit less than half of these conflicts.

On the basis of the general and organisational attributes noted above, two principal patterns of industrial action can be distinguished; these may be referred to as the *sectional autonomy*[15] and *mass solidarity* profiles respectively.

According to Table 3.3, 67.9 per cent of total work stoppages are of the sectional autonomy kind. These are restricted to single work-units whose members generally, though not invariably, also belong to the same union. Conflicts of this kind, most often strikes or stop-work meetings, do not persist for long: only a small proportion (17.5 per cent) go beyond two days. The most common issues precipitating sectional action include disability and special allowance payments and matters concerning manning, allocation of labour, dismissals, and discipline. Trade union issues are also significant, with stoppages related to demarcation and intra-union communications (stop-work or branch meetings). Finally, as the term sectional autonomy implies, these disputes are mobilised by work-unit members and job delegates, though in some cases full-time officials may also play a role.

The mass solidarity industrial action pattern is typified by a smaller number of large scale disputes (23.4 per cent) based on inter-union co-operation at both the job delegate and union official level. These stoppages are of short duration, but, unlike their sectional counterparts, they focus on improvements in basic pay and conditions, the plight of the industry, and wider political issues.

Explaining the Patterns of Industrial Action

The previous section outlined the two dominant types of disputes; it is now necessary to provide an explanation for their presence in the ship-building industry. These will be considered in turn, beginning with the sectional autonomy pattern.

The Sectional Autonomy Industrial Action Pattern

The demand for shipbuilding and shiprepair work is highly unstable, despite the fact that subsidies and government contracts in naval yards reduce some of the fluctuations.[16] Nevertheless, even in the more favourably placed naval sub-sector, the Committee of Enquiry into Industrial Relations in Naval Dockyards pointed out that work levels for the different occupations undertaking vessel refits 'vary from one period to the next and more often than not it is impossible for refit planners to arrange sufficient capacity in times of peak workloads and then avoid the dilemma of excess capacity at other times' (1975: 20–21).

Variations in demand for labour affect workers' earnings and hence their economic and psychological well-being. There is a tendency for work-units to use every opportunity to increase earnings in order to make up for periods when only the base rate is applicable.[17] This is facilitated by unit production and the nature of customer contracts. New orders entail the revision of decisions on manning levels, allowances, and disability rates; a short stoppage, or even a stop-work meeting, at a critical time can substantially improve the rewards of the relevant work-unit. Such opportunities arise immediately prior to the disbursement of progress payments when the firm's cash flow position is weak, when the demand for the labour of a particular occupational group is necessary for the continuity of production, and as the delivery date approaches. At these points in the production cycle industrial action goes hand in hand with fractional bargaining (Chamberlain and Kuhn, 1965: 259–263).

Employers use a variety of adjustment strategies to limit the imbalances between labour supply and demand.[18] In periods of excess demand, overtime working, sub-contracting, and labour 'borrowing' are options that have been used; labour hoarding and diversification of activity are two means of coping with excess supply. Use of overtime can lead to conflict over earnings relativities. Unions have sought control over overtime rotas in order to ensure an equitable distribution of overtime work. This in turn contributes to conflict with management who wish to allocate overtime strictly in accordance with production requirements. A management document highlights this problem as follows:

> The use of unofficial overtime rosters . . . makes it extremely difficult to allocate overtime according to work requirements . . . Some employees not only seek to achieve absolute equality but claim that equality should be across sections and whole [production groups].

Sub-contracting and labour 'borrowing' are not favoured by shipyard workers for two main reasons: the former option reduces the potential for overtime earnings and, even when a specific skill is in short supply, agreeing to the use of sub-contract labour can lead to a permanent loss of work in the future. These adjustment practices can give rise to serious demarcation disputes as workers attempt to appropriate all work that is available. A notable case summarised from the Weekly Reports involved fifty-seven ETU members who ceased work for three weeks in protest at the redundancy of workers in the same union while contractors were still employed at the yard in question.

Labour hoarding is common where retention of scarce industry skills is desired, though it encourages variable work effort norms and inconsistencies in supervisory practices.

Diversification is popular as a means of achieving employment stability. One naval yard has become involved in bridge construction, and most commercial establishments perform various kinds of engineering work. A combination of shipbuilding and shiprepair also helps to reduce fluctuations in the demand for labour. But not all occupations lend themselves to diversification. This leads to relativity problems, since the skills of workers such as metal and building tradesmen are more universal than those of coppersmiths, shipwrights, and painters and dockers. Indeed, in the case of painters and dockers there is a proportion of casual employees for whom high employment and earnings instability are facts of life (see Royal Commission into Alleged Payments to Maritime Unions, 1976: 31, 121-2).

Several authors have noted the impact of product market fluctuations on shipbuilding industrial relations (see Cameron, 1964: 7; Alexander and Jenkins, 1970: 40-41; Commission on Industrial Relations, 1971: 102-4; and R. K. Brown et al., 1972: 29-30). But it is also important to stress the way in which labour adjustment strategies on the one hand cushion the adverse effects of work and earnings instability, but, on the other, create new sources of conflict between management and workers. In any event, work instability does not by itself explain the specific features of industrial action in the shipbuilding industry. This requires an appreciation of the interaction between product and labour market influences, the system of production, the division of labour, union structure, and accommodation arrangements.

In the first section of this chapter attention was drawn to the nature of shipbuilding production processes in which various occupational groups perform specialised work tasks in a sequential manner. Here it should be emphasised that craft administration of production requires substantial work-unit autonomy (Stinchcombe, 1959: 173); this accords with the stress placed on unilateral regulation by craft unions generally (Aldridge, 1976: 8-25; Goodrich, 1975: 264) and by semi-skilled unions in the shipbuilding industry. Work-unit cohesion is buttressed by the shared experience of variations in market pressure according to the stage in the production cycle. Powerlessness at the hands of market forces in one period gives way to a measure of job and earnings control at other times.

Trade union structure in shipbuilding originally developed out of the highly differentiated division of labour (Webb, 1919: 508-9); it remains much the same despite several union amalgamations.[19] Indeed, the conciliation and arbitration system and consecutive governments have done little to encourage union mergers,[20] so the contours of trade unionism are still by and large compatible with various occupational boundaries. However, as noted earlier, the great majority of unions have only a small proportion of their total membership in the shipbuilding industry. These two aspects of union structure have several important consequences for industrial relations.

In the first place, occupational boundaries and custom and practice rules concerning manning, work allocation, discipline, and work effort are legitimised by the trade unions in the immediate interests of their members and on the grounds of organisational survival. This makes for inevitable and uncompromising conflict with management. Secondly, inter-union competition is exacerbated, and constructive co-operation made more difficult, by the existence of occupational unions.[21] This is well attested by the large number and broad-based nature of demarcation struggles in this industry. On the basis of data drawn from one major commercial yard for the period 1969–76, sixty-eight disputes of this kind were reported. Nearly half involved conflict between unions representing workers with similar levels of skill, a quarter included unions whose members' skill levels differed, and a further quarter involved disputes between unions and sub-contractors, or non-union personnel allegedly performing union members' work.[22]

There is a strong tendency then for trade unions to accentuate rather than minimise occupational differentiation, so it is extremely difficult to improve productivity through changes in work practices.

Union structure discourages efficient representation and rapid resolution of members' problems. With the exception of the FSPDU and the AMWSU, the full-time officials of most other unions have little time to devote to the problems of their members in the shipbuilding industry since these constitute such a small fraction of total union membership. In addition, the unique nature of the industry, with its many custom and practice rules and informal agreements, means that few union officials are closely acquainted with the key issues. Matters must be left in the hands of job delegates whose training and experience is very uneven.

The problem of reconciling rank and file demands with union policy is essentially resolved by the endorsement or pragmatic acceptance by officials of rank and file activity based on custom and practice norms. In general, union officials are unable to exert control over sectional action except through persuasion at stop-work meetings and indirectly by exercising some influence on shop committee executives. In any case, most officials accept the right of specific union groups to take industrial action so long as this activity does not seriously jeopardise the employment of their members. There is, therefore, considerable pressure on work-units to restrict the duration of their stoppages.

Unit production, craft administration, and craft unionism are interrelated, and, together with an unstable product market, these features of the industry have contributed to the strength of the second, decentralised tier of the accommodation structure. The informal nature of much workplace industrial relations is further accentuated by weak management control systems that reflect the influence of traditional craft autonomy. In addition, the unsophisticated management approach to industrial relations is especially important in the naval sub-sector, where formal decision-making is highly centralised and there is a high turnover of managers. This formal system is frequently undermined by a network of informal arrangements that facilitate job delegate bargaining particularly in respect of manning, effort, and allowances in periods of peak labour demand. Upholding the craft union norm of direct democracy, delegates rarely make decisions on behalf of their colleagues. Usually sectional stop-work meetings provide a forum for worker decision-making. Such meetings are also used to pressure management for further concessions, and they also have the unintended consequence of reinforcing a sectional bargaining awareness (W. A. Brown, 1973: 173–4; Batstone et al., 1977: 56).

To round off this discussion, it may be useful to illustrate the relationships between the factors that promote sectionalism by reference to the most militant union group — the Painters and Dockers (FSPDU).These workers perform a variety of semi-skilled and unskilled tasks including hull scraping, sandblasting, painting, scaffold erection, and operation of floating cranes. There are about 2000 members in this union, all of whom work in the shipbuilding industry, most of them engaged on repair work. Painters and dockers constitute a work-unit since, in nearly all yards, they use separate amenity blocks or worksheds. The men mostly work in small, single union groups, which, along with a common union experience and a shared reputation for toughness and commercial astuteness, fosters social cohesion. Up to 20 per cent of these workers are casual employees engaged through a union 'pick-up' system.[23] This arrangement further encourages a positive orientation to the union. The small number of painters and dockers also aids union solidarity.

The FSPDU has adopted many of the conventions of craft unionism. Aspiring members must 'walk the floor' before gaining admission, and, once accepted, they become subject to rigidly enforced rules on voting, union decision-making, and worker behaviour. Regular quarterly branch meetings are held in working hours, contributing to the high incidence of short stoppages attributed to intra-union communication (see Table 3.2).

Union officials are especially close to the members. The small number of workplaces located in harbour areas, with union offices nearby, makes for frequent personal contact between FSPDU officials and the rank and file. By and large the union officers defend the militant sectionalism of their members because, like many craft unions, technological change in the form of mechanised sandblasting and painting techniques and more durable protective hull coatings has reduced the volume of work available to members. Moreover, the FSPDU finds itself in a declining industry with little chance of membership expansion, since union jurisdictional boundaries are well established. Faced with these problems, members and officials of the FSPDU jealously guard their work from management interference and from the control of members of other unions. This sometimes leads to complicated disputes, for example:

The FSPDU imposed bans on work associated with the ... dredge crane ... in support of claims for the right of FSPDU to do rigging work for metal tradesmen on the crane. The company had allocated this work to the FIA. (Weekly Reports, Department of Employment and Industrial Relations, 1977)

Based on demarcation dispute data referred to earlier (*supra* p.77), the FSPDU was found to be involved in 41.3 per cent of these conflicts, the highest participation rate of all the unions. This is not simply an indicator of defensiveness; expansion of job territory is a related objective of the FSPDU. Job consciousness, rule-oriented behaviour, and militancy are interconnected as the following statement, obtained in an interview with a member of the union, makes clear:

The Painters and Dockers are a powerful union because they are close knit and run by men who stuck to the rules they made. These rules are as old as shipbuilding. They would not release work that was theirs — they used their power to preserve this [control].

The Painters and Dockers not only engage in industrial action in support of job control issues (recorded in Table 3.2 under the broad headings of 'manning and work allocation' and 'demarcation'), but also over pay. Concentration is less on base rates than on overtime and the array of supplementary payments and allowances that are paid in the industry. Work-units engage in bargaining and associated industrial action at strategic points of the production cycle and the gains that are made are rarely subject to the 'flow-on' process. This fractional bargaining boosts members' earnings as well as helping to ensure that these workers do not leave the industry or join another union. It is one way in which the union can legitimate its existence as a separate organisation.

How different are painters and dockers from other unionists in shipbuilding? Can they really be regarded as exemplars of the sectional autonomy dispute pattern? There are several distinguishing features of the FSPDU that contribute to the greater militancy of these workers but do not alter the essentially sectionalist nature of their industrial struggles.[24] These characteristics, which have been referred to in the course of the discussion are: the small size and dependence of the union on the industry, the significant proportion of casual workers in the organisation, the proximity of union leaders to the rank and file, and, perhaps most importantly, the greater social cohesion of this occupational group.[25] In sum, the Painters and Dockers provide a typical example of the characteristics that contribute to the sectional autonomy pattern.

Two final observations on the sectional character of industrial disputes should be made. Firstly, the multi-union variant, which accounts for 11.2

per cent of stoppages (see Table 3.3), largely reflects the composition of metal trades work-units. It is common for AMWSU boilermakers, FIA tradesmen's assistants, and occasionally ASE fitters to work alongside one another.[26] Accordingly, members of more than one union are typically involved in sectional action. The mobilisers of industrial action in these instances are nearly always AMWSU stewards.

The second point is that management have increasingly come to realise that in the interests of increased productivity work-units must be subject to greater regulation. The potential role of shop committee executives as 'managers of discontent' (Mills, 1948: 6) and guardians of agreements has been recognised, but this tendency to legitimise and formalise the role of workplace union organisation has not proceeded very far. Indeed, on issues of trade union principle, for example, dismissals, discipline, and safety, shop committee executives have themselves acted as mobilisers of industrial action. But apart from these instances, which account for only 7.0 per cent of disputes (see Table 3.3), action is confined to single work-units on the one hand and much larger collectivities on the other.

The Mass Solidarity Industrial Action Pattern

Large scale campaign and protest actions in the shipbuilding industry represent wider orbits of solidarity. This type of activity is less common since the division of labour and union structure impede the development of working class unity. Yet as Hyman points out:

> sectional and class consciousness are not mutually exclusive alternatives. Awareness of common class identity is constituted out of consciousness of sectional interests; it does not presuppose the elimination of sectional loyalties and identification. (1978: 66)

This view receives some support from the survey data referred to earlier. An index of traditional proletarian imagery (Lockwood, 1966: 250–2) was constructed, and the survey results indicated that one-third of the sample held such a view of society. This figure is relatively high by comparison with other studies (Goldthorpe et al., 1968: 145–50; Cousins and R. K. Brown, 1975: 68).[27]

There are several factors that encourage a wider solidarity among shipbuilding workers. Common and related awards and agreements foster inter-union co-operation; so do problems that affect all workers more or less simultaneously. The decline of the industry is a good example of this type of issue. National political decisions provide a further opportunity for officials and members of different unions to unite.

Shipbuilding awards and agreements are associated with the general system of conciliation and arbitration through a network of arrangements, the most important of which is the Metal Industry Award. This covers major groups of metalworkers employed in commercial shipbuilding establishments as well as in many other enterprises in the manufacturing sector. Because of its centrality, improvements achieved in the Metal Industry Award constitute an important precedent within the arbitration system for gains in related awards. Thus metalworkers in all but the most peripheral industries are required by their unions (chiefly the AMWSU, ASE, and FIA) to demonstrate support for improvements in this award. These typically take the form of twenty-four hour State or nation-wide stoppages as part of campaigns orchestrated by Metal Trades Federation officials[28] in conjunction with job delegate committees.

Officials and delegates of the AMWSU usually play a key leadership role in these and other multi-union campaign actions. This union is well known for its militancy, and as the largest in the industry, it is favourably placed to take advantage of its pivotal position. Although the FIA is also involved in many multi-union campaign actions, officials and delegates of this union generally follow the lead given by the AMWSU. FIA and ASE officials are regarded as moderates and are much more inclined to react to events, in contrast to the AMWSU, whose officials plan and mobilise in anticipation of management and government policy changes.

The nexus between the Metal Industry Award and the shipbuilding industry in Sydney has been diminished by the Port of Sydney Agreement. This has encouraged multi-union campaign action on a regional basis when periodic, usually annual, negotiations take place. The economic recession has limited militant action in the same way as the onset of high unemployment and indexation in 1975 restricted specific district and yard campaigns for improvements in local agreements.

The severe downturn in the shipbuilding industry, coupled with the declining level of protection available since 1973, has led to a succession of yard closures and large scale redundancies (Aungles and Szelenyi, 1979). The unions have responded by taking mass protest action, occasionally restricted to specific yards (especially over redundancy settlements), and at other times involving the whole industry. The prime objectives of union officials and yard committees have been to alert the community to the human and social costs of reduced protection and to influence the Government to reverse its import and subsidy policies. Street marches, deputations to Federal Ministers, and the establishment of joint worker-community committees were, however, unsuccessful in obtaining a greater measure of protection for the industry.

Finally, shipbuilding workers also take part in national political protest actions, such as those against the dismissal of the Labor Government in 1975 and the subsequent dismantling of the national health scheme (Medibank). Thus, although sectional struggles are the norm, a strong working class tradition among shipbuilding workers means that solidarity of a wider kind is possible, though it rarely finds expression in the form of protracted trials of strength.

Conclusion

Two dominant industrial action patterns have been identified in the ship-building industry. The sectional autonomy profile reflects pressures exerted by work-units at the point of production. The high incidence and fragmented nature of bargaining at this level owes much to an unstable product market, the complex division of labour based on craft adminis-tration principles, and the impact of craft unionism. By contrast, the mass solidarity pattern represents a concentration of labour pressure on a wider front, directed at issues and problems that shipbuilding workers share in common: basic award and agreement conditions, the prospect and reality of mass unemployment, and the behaviour of governments.

The evidence presented in this chapter suggests that job delegates play a mobilising role, with respect to both sectional and mass solidarity stoppages. Does this mean that the further development of workplace organisation is likely to promote or inhibit orderly industrial relations? The answer seems to be that things will be much the same as before; it is difficult to see how shop committees and their executives can substan-tially augment their authority. Members of work-units and union officials are reluctant to compromise their autonomy, while management lack the determination and resources to reform workplace industrial relations.

The shipbuilding industry epitomises the force of tradition. This is illustrated by our frequent use of the term craft, which has been employed in connection with the method of production, the division of labour, and trade unionism. Why has there been so little change in this industry? Is it really the workers and the unions who must bear responsibility for decline and unemployment? The answer appears to be that there has been insufficient incentive for management to undertake investment in new plant and equipment and to reform business and industrial relations practices.[29] Management optimism has never been high, given the limited size of domestic markets and a continual fear of exposure to strong overseas competition. This has ensured the continuity of tradition with its comparatively inefficient work practices. Inferior industrial relations are more a symptom than a cause of decline.

Unfortunately it is difficult to be enthusiastic about the future of Australia's shipbuilding and repair industry.

NOTES

1.   This study is being undertaken by the author in collaboration with Mr E. J. Burke with support from the Reserve Bank of Australia.

2. A detailed outline of protection policies is contained in successive Tariff Board and Industries Assistance Commission Reports. A useful historical summary appears in the Tariff Board Report on the industry in 1971.
3. This estimate is based on private information from the Department of Industry and Commerce.
4. The extent of recession in the industry is highlighted by figures contained in the 1978 Annual Report of Lloyd's Register of Shipping which show that between 1973 and 1978 world orders dropped from 75 to 9 million gross tonnes.
5. Employment information was obtained from the Department of Defence.
6. This estimate was supplied by the Department of Industry and Commerce.
7. Aggregate industry employment figures have been derived from various issues of ABS, Catalogue no.8202.0.
8. This Agreement, which is registered in the AC&AC, resulted from protracted negotiations between unions and employers, with encouragement from the Tribunal member assigned to the industry.
9. Because naval dockyards operate under defence legislation, they fall within the jurisdiction of the Public Service Arbitration system. The specific instrument that applies in these cases is designated Determination no.44 of 1955.
10. The Agreement makes reference to the possibility of special site rates being agreed to in certain instances.
11. An average of 6.4 strikes per month was recorded by the ABS, and 6.0 in the Weekly Reports.
12. An important task of some industrial officers in larger yards is to record dispute details. It is not uncommon to find commencement and cessation times of stoppages stated to the nearest minute.
13. Longer duration stoppages are a crude barometer of the intensity of conflict. In this regard, it is significant to note that FSPDU members were involved in two-fifths of stoppages extending for ten days or more, a proportion well above that of any other union.
14. The reason for including yard-wide and multi-yard disputes in one category is that these struggles have much in common, and, given the dispersed nature of the industry, establishment-wide actions are frequently substitutes for more widespread activity.
15. This term is used by Frenkel (1978a: 394) to describe characteristics of the dispute pattern in the Pilbara iron ore industry.
16. A useful account of influences on the demand for ships is given in Parkinson (1960).
17. It is estimated, in an unpublished Department of Defence report, that in 1975 workers at naval dockyards earned about $400 a year through special allowances. This amounted to approximately 6 per cent of base wage rates.
18. Some industrial relations consequences of labour market adjustment strategies are detailed in B. Thomas and D. Deaton (1978).
19. In the early seventies the Amalgamated Metal Workers' Union was formed by the amalgamation of the Boilermakers' and Blacksmiths' Society, the Sheet Metal Working Industrial Union, and the Amalgamated Engineers' Union. In 1976, the FSSCA (Federated Shipwrights and Ship Constructors' Association of Australia) joined this group to form the AMWSU.
20. Section 158N of the Conciliation and Arbitration Act (1904–80) requires that for each organisation involved, at least 50 per cent of members return ballot papers and that at least 50 per cent of formal votes cast approve amalgamation.
21. The Naval Work Adjustment Agreement negotiated in 1969 was a limited productivity bargain designed to introduce more flexible job boundaries in naval yards. Department of Defence officials maintain that this agreement has not been very successful.

22. An instructive analysis of shipbuilding demarcation disputes is provided by Eldridge (1968). Details of demarcation rules and procedures in the British industry, many of which are paralleled in Australia, are contained in Roberts (1967).
23. When casual labour is required by employers they inform the union secretary. He then 'picks-up' the required number of workers from those who attend the union office seeking work on the day in question.
24. Painters and dockers might be regarded in some senses as 'all round militants'. That they are not averse to multi-union action is shown by their involvement in 56.6 per cent of these stoppages (see Table 3.4).
25. Shipwrights share some of these distinguishing characteristics.
26. The ASE does not have members in all major yards.
27. The incidence of a traditional proletarian image of society among specific groups was greatest among painters and dockers, job delegates, and plumbers. In the first and second cases this is consistent with the data on painter and docker militancy and with the mobilisation role of delegates. In the case of plumbers it is likely that their considerable exposure to demarcation struggles at the yard in question strongly influenced their perceptions of society.
28. The Metal Trades Federation is a loose organisation of unions with membership in the metal industries. Its major aim is to co-ordinate action for improvements in the Metal Industry Award. AMWSU officials tend to play a key role in the formulation of policy, strategy and tactics.
29. This contrasts with the situation in some overseas countries, for example Sweden. Developments at Kockums shipyard in the early seventies are of interest (see Report of Australian Shipbuilding Industry Study Mission, 1975: 100–102).

CHAPTER FOUR

Change and Conflict on the Waterfront*

Don J. Turkington

Within the span of a dozen years the face of the docks has changed dramatically. Giant terminals now stand where once only thistles flourished, and machines have increasingly replaced men. Individual handling has given way to containers, bulk loaders, and unit cargoes. Not all this change has been smooth. In New Zealand, as elsewhere, some of the change has been accompanied by conflict.

New Zealand's 18 ports ring its two main islands and range in size from Auckland with 1300 watersiders to Greymouth with only eleven. Waterside workers total about 5000 nationally and form by far the largest occupational group in the industry.[1] Their work involves the loading and unloading of vessels and, in some cases, the moving of cargo across the wharf. Waterside workers are all union members and belong to local port unions that are affiliated to the New Zealand Waterside Workers' Federation (NZWWF). This port structure of unions has its origin in one of New Zealand's most historic industrial disputes, the 1951 waterfront dispute (see Bassett, 1972).

Prior to 1951 watersiders were organised into a national union, the New Zealand Waterside Workers' Union (NZWWU). This highly active and Communist-led union entered into a dispute with employers over wages in early February 1951. The employers' 'final offer' was rejected as inadequate by the NZWWU, and a national overtime ban was imposed. The response of the employers was to threaten a suspension of two days for every one day worked while the overtime ban remained in force. At this early stage the Government became involved and pressured watersiders to lift their ban on overtime. The employers then stepped up their

*Special thanks are due to Brian Wood of the Waterfront Industry Commission who commented on earlier drafts of this chapter. Responsibility for the contents of the paper lies with the author.

action by making the availability of work 'subject to the acceptance of normal hours of work including overtime if required' (quoted in Bassett, 1972: 76). The men saw themselves as locked out, and New Zealand's most traumatic dispute began in earnest.

During the five months of the dispute, the Government assumed almost unlimited powers, which included the use of the armed services on the wharves and the suspension of civil liberties in the case of waterside workers. The Government was determined to break the NZWWU and in the process deregistered the union. This meant that the union was dissolved as a legal entity and that watersiders were no longer recognised as belonging to a union. Should a new union receive government permission to become registered, watersiders seeking a job would be forced by the compulsory unionism provisions of the conciliation and arbitration law to join that union. The Government's aim was to replace the national NZWWU with autonomous port unions and to ensure that members of the former union for the most part did not join any of the new unions. In this it was largely successful, for by the end of the dispute twenty-six small unions existed in place of the one national waterside workers' union. While experienced watersiders were not slow in gaining control of these port unions, even to this day they have failed to re-form into a national union. The New Zealand Waterside Workers' Federation is the best they have achieved in developing a unified organisational structure.

While belonging to this national federation, the port unions are largely autonomous. Each union conducts its own local business and can make its own rules providing they are not inconsistent with those of the NZWWF. In practice, links between the port unions and the NZWWF are close, with ports looking to the Federation for guidance and assistance on many matters.

The principal officers of the NZWWF (president, vice-president, general secretary, and assistant general secretary) are elected every two years through a national ballot of the membership of all port unions. The general secretary and assistant general secretary are full-time officials. All port unions have annual elections for president, vice-president, secretary, treasurer, and other members of the committee of management or the executive. At the larger ports one or more of these officers is full-time. Among the members of the committee of management is usually an official (termed a 'walking delegate' or 'disputes officer') who represents the union in the event of a dispute anywhere in the port. Most ports have a delegate system but this varies considerably. In some cases the union officials and executive members perform this role, while in others rank and file workers are elected delegates for the duration of a particular job.

Employers of waterside labour are mainly stevedoring companies, which, in turn, work mostly for overseas shipping lines. Many of these lines are associated through shipping conferences or cartels that are concerned with fixing freight rates, obtaining and sharing cargoes, and the like. The major shipping companies also own numerous subsidiaries, among which are important stevedoring companies. Most 'independent' New Zealand stevedoring companies operate at only one or a few ports.

The vast majority of employers of waterfront labour belong to the New Zealand Waterside Employers' Industrial Union of Employers (NZWEU). The management of this national organisation lies with a management committee that is elected annually. Its administrative head is the general secretary who is an appointed official. Within the NZWEU are sixteen port branches whose structure follows that of the national body, with a branch secretary (in some branches full-time), a committee of management, and so on. Branch offices have limited autonomy, as they are bound by any decision of the national management committee or of the NZWEU's general meeting. Moreover, a branch committee is not able to enter into negotiation on matters of other than local significance, nor can it do so in respect of wages and conditions without prior approval of the national management committee. Disputes are frequently referred by the employer or employers involved to the national or branch officers of the NZWEU for settlement.

The operators of New Zealand's four container terminals have formed themselves into an incorporated society called the New Zealand Container Terminal Operators' Association. This association represents employers in container terminal negotiations.

Like other employers, New Zealand waterfront employers are responsible for supervising the work of their employees. But unlike other employers, few of their workers are permanent employees. Instead, waterside workers are allocated to them by a statutory body — the Waterfront Industry Commission (WIC) — which performs many functions that in other industries would be undertaken by the employer. The origins of the WIC date back to 1940, when a commission was established in an effort to introduce some regularity into a very unstable employment situation. Today the Commission is a representative organisation, consisting of a neutral chairman, a representative from each of the NZWEU and the New Zealand Harbour Boards' Industrial Union of Employers, and two representatives of the NZWWF. Its wide-ranging functions are set out in the Waterfront Industry Act, 1976 and include: determining the appropriate number of workers at each port; registering employers, who, as a result, become entitled to employ waterside labour; engaging and allocating waterside workers; paying wages, allowances, and other payments; and providing amenities for watersiders. The engagement and allocation function is complex and operates as follows: employers requiring labour lodge a requisition with the local labour engagement bureau of the WIC stating the number of gangs of men required for a ship or job, the class of work, and the time the men are required to start. The bureau attempts to ensure that hours worked are equalised among waterside workers and as a result men with the lowest hours recorded receive the first available job. Once labour has been allocated to an employer, the men come under the direct control of the employer who, through his superintendents and foreman stevedores, is responsible for supervision. The men are allocated to gangs that exist only for the duration of a job. The exceptions are the container terminals, where workers are assigned for up to twenty-four weeks before being rotated back to other work, and the roll-on – roll-off terminals, where they are assigned for twelve weeks. Employers must accept the workers allocated to them.

Most of the WIC's functions are administrative in character; the business of dispute settlement is handled by a separate structure. Just as the WIC is a unique body within New Zealand industry, so also is the waterfront's system of conciliation and arbitration. The Government long ago hived this highly problematic industry off from the general law on conciliation and arbitration, providing instead specific institutions through the Waterfront Industry Acts of 1953 and 1976. At the national level is a conciliation council consisting of a neutral chairman and an equal number of workers' representatives (from the NZWWF) and of employers' representatives (seven from the NZWEU and one from the New Zealand Harbour Boards Employers' Union in recent negotiations). It is the job of the chairman to assist the parties to reach a settlement on new national awards or general principal orders. Matters that can't be decided on by consent go to the arbitration body – the Waterfront Industry Tribunal – which makes a ruling that, together with the already agreed sections, is issued as an award. Among other matters that go to the Tribunal are demarcation disputes, disputes not settled at the local level, and appeals from decisions of local dispute settlement bodies. The Tribunal consists of a judge of the Arbitration Court and two other members who effectively represent workers and employers in the industry.

At the port level are port conciliation committees, which consist of a neutral chairman and an equal number of representatives of employers and workers. The port conciliation committee assists the parties in making local agreements or awards (called supplementary principal orders) as part of its general brief to settle local disputes. The committee is very flexible and can meet at short notice.

Among occupational groups closely connected with waterside workers are shipwrights and tally clerks. Shipwrights perform carpentry work and have recently amalgamated with waterside workers' unions. The work of tallying, or counting cargo, is performed by tally clerks who have also recently merged with watersiders' unions at several ports.

A feature of the New Zealand waterfront is that most of the mechanical equipment on conventional wharves, such as cranes and other vehicles, is owned by harbour boards and operated by their employees. In the case of container terminals, the only cargo handling job exclusively performed by harbour board employees is the operation of the shipside portainer cranes. All other cargo work, including the driving of vehicles, is undertaken by 'composite workforces' composed in the ratio of six waterside workers to every one harbour board employee. Roll-on – roll-off terminals, with one exception, are worked exclusively by waterside workers.

All harbour board employees, including the minority concerned with cargo handling, belong to the New Zealand Harbour Boards Employees' Union. This national union covers a very wide range of occupations from clerical workers through to tradesmen. Its 15 branches have a total membership of 3000, of which about 1000 are concerned with cargo handling. Many of the latter, however, are not engaged full-time in cargo handling but alternate between that and other types of work according to the demand.

The harbour boards themselves are elected local authorities charged with the management of New Zealand's harbours, and as employers are grouped into the New Zealand Harbour Boards' Industrial Union of Employers. For most purposes, industrial relations in harbour boards are conducted not within the special framework applicable to waterside workers but under the general system of conciliation and arbitration prescribed in the Industrial Relations Act, 1973. Their cargo handling sections, however, are increasingly coming within the orbit of the Waterfront Industry Act, 1976.

In addition to harbour board employees, another occupational group permanently located on the waterfront is that of foreman stevedores, who are the permanent supervision staff of stevedoring and shipping companies. Foreman stevedores belong to port branches of the New Zealand Foreman Stevedores', Timekeepers' and Permanent Hands' Union. In the vicinity of the wharf are to be found storemen and packers, and on a temporary and intermittent basis, drivers, seamen, and railway workers.

Patterning of Industrial Action

The statistical activities of the Waterfront Industry Commission ensure that the data on industrial action for the waterfront are the best of any New Zealand industry. Other industries do not have the benefit of a statutory body charged with overseeing and reporting their operations. As a result, the stoppage levels of these other industries are under-stated relative to those of the waterfront. But even the WIC has its limits, and some of the very shortest and smallest disputes go unreported and the

Commission only reports disputes involving waterside workers, with the exception of harbour board employees engaged in cargo handling, although they are much less important than watersiders in the overall pattern of industrial action.[2] While other groups are not ignored, our emphasis in this chapter is on the main occupational group in the industry, namely, waterside workers. Statistics used are those of the WIC and cover the decade 1969–78. This period embraces the introduction of containers and other changes in technology, thereby enabling the relationship between change and conflict to be explored.

TABLE 4.1

Industrial action by number of workers involved, New Zealand waterfront industry, 1969–78

Number of workers involved	Number of disputes %	Workers involved %	Working days 'lost' %
Under 50	6.7	0.2	0.3
50 and under 100	7.7	0.7	0.3
100 and under 200	8.7	1.5	1.6
200 and under 400	14.4	5.5	4.5
400 and under 1000	34.4	26.9	26.5
1000 and under 2000	23.1	40.0	33.5
2000 and under 3000	2.1	6.7	6.5
3000 and over	3.1	18.5	26.7
Total	100.2*	100.0	99.9*
Number of disputes, workers, days 'lost'	195	158 171	136 813

*Figures do not add up to 100 because of rounding off figures.

Source: Derived from Waterfront Industry Commission data.

Over the decade 1969-78 New Zealand waterside workers engaged in an average of 19.5 disputes a year, most of which were large in terms of the numbers of workers involved in them. Table 4.1 shows that nearly 63 per cent involved 400 or more workers. This reflects the fact that the vast majority of waterfront disputes cover all watersiders at a port. Table 4.2 gives a breakdown according to organisational scope, which confirms that sectional stoppages by work groups, such as gangs, are rare on the New Zealand waterfront.

TABLE 4.2

Industrial disputes by organisational scope, New Zealand waterfront industry, 1969–78

Organisational scope	Number of disputes %
Ship	12.8
Terminal or terminals	4.6
Port	75.9
Several ports	3.6
National	3.1
Total	100.0
Number of disputes	195

Source: Derived from Waterfront Industry Commission data.

The very short duration of disputes on the waterfront can be seen from Table 4.3. More than 40 per cent of disputes last four hours or less and nearly three-quarters are over within a day. Stoppages on the waterfront are even briefer than in other New Zealand industries where the average duration is measured in days rather than hours. While this may partly reflect the better recording of disputes by the WIC, it also reflects an important aspect of disputes in the industry.

Over a third (35 per cent) of all disputes on the waterfront are 'unauthorised' stop-work meetings, a proportion that is much higher than in most other industries. Waterside workers are entitled to a monthly two-hour stop-work meeting under their agreement but have a considerable capacity to extend these authorised meetings or to hold other, unauthorised ones. Strikes, of course, also figure prominently, accounting for 62 per cent of disputes over the period under discussion. Of the remaining 3 per cent, most were 'penalties' consisting of suspension of the labour force by employers in retaliation for a stoppage of work. In New Zealand ports, 'bureau rules' provide for penalties to be imposed on workers who infringe certain work rules.

While we have broken down disputes according to various dimensions this is to some extent arbitrary. Disputes are sometimes difficult to categorise, as the following illustration shows. A bonus rate dispute at the port of Mount Maunganui led workers to hold two stop-work meetings and then refuse to work the vessels of the employer concerned. These men were placed on penalty and other workers transferred to the ships that had been given a 'preference for labour' status by employers. As the other workers refused the work, they too were placed on penalty.

TABLE 4.3

Industrial action by duration, New Zealand waterfront industry,
1969–78

Duration (working days)	Number of disputes %	Workers involved %	Working days 'lost' %
Up to 4 hours	43.1	40.1	11.1
Over 4 hours to 1 day	29.7	27.0	26.7
Over 1 to 2 days	15.4	21.4	30.2
Over 2 to 3 days	4.1	6.2	13.2
Over 3 to less than 5 days	2.1	2.3	7.2
5 days and over	5.6	3.0	11.6
Total	100.0	100.0	100.0
Number of disputes, workers, days 'lost'	195	158 171	136 813

Source: Derived from Waterfront Industry Commission data.

WIC statistics are largely confined to stoppages of work although more important restrictions on output are mentioned in its annual report. Bans of various sorts are quite common on the New Zealand waterfront. They have been placed on new types of vessels and equipment, on containers handled by other workers, on flags of convenience vessels, on French shipping during periods of nuclear testing, and so on. Go slows and working to rule are less common, while unofficial strikes are unknown. The importance of bans, stop-work meetings, and official strikes was confirmed by management and union responses to a recent questionnaire (Turkington, 1976: 251).

The complexity of disputes also means that any classification of them according to issue must be treated with caution. Table 4.4 reveals that disputes on the New Zealand waterfront arise over a wide range of issues, prominent among which are award or agreement claims. Award disputes are not only relatively numerous but also large and long. Stoppages involving union business are also numerous and large, but being mainly stop-work meetings, are of short duration. Demarcation disputes are common as are stoppages over social or political issues. Disputes over allowances and special rates tend to involve only one ship and, while being reasonably common, are short and involve few workers. Watersiders are clearly interested in gaining the highest possible reward for their efforts and in safeguarding work they consider their own. They are not reluctant to protest over social and political matters nor to deal with union business through stop-work meetings.

TABLE 4.4

Industrial disputes by cited issue, New Zealand waterfront industry,
1969–78

Cited Issue	Number of disputes %	Workers involved %	Working days 'lost' %
Wages:			
Allowance & special rates	9.2	2.7	3.2
Award or agreement claims	14.4	25.0	37.3
Hours of work	2.1	1.3	0.5
Leave, pensions etc	1.5	5.5	5.6
Managerial policy	9.7	5.8	3.9
Physical working conditions:			
Safety	3.6	1.5	1.7
Working conditions	4.6	2.7	3.8
Trade unionism:			
Demarcation	13.3	9.6	12.3
Sympathy	2.6	1.0	0.7
Union business	14.4	18.4	6.7
Social, political	12.8	14.3	15.2
Other	11.8	12.2	9.2
Total	100.0	100.0	100.1*
Number of disputes, workers, days 'lost'	195	158 171	136 813

*Figures do not add up to 100 due to rounding off figures.

Source: Derived from Waterfront Industry Commission data.

Watersiders are unusual among New Zealand workers in effectively having 'plant' unions. Each port has its own union, the offices and leadership of which are located in the wharf area. Some officials are full-time and, as previously noted, several ports actually have an official (the walking delegate) designated to represent the union in disputes. The rules of some port unions provide that disputes will be considered by the union executive and, if need be, by a meeting of members. In the meantime, members continue working. In a situation so well served by union officials, it is not surprising that they are the leaders in strike situations.

There is some variation in dispute-proneness among the ports. The four largest ports (Auckland, Mount Maunganui, Wellington, and Lyttelton) accounted for three-quarters of all disputes over the decade, although they employed just 62 per cent of the total labour force. Other large ports experienced considerable industrial action. On the other hand, some of the small ports obviously experience very few stoppages.

In most years, the waterfront figures among the half-dozen industries with the highest dispute levels in New Zealand (Turkington, 1977b). In historical terms the last decade has seen moderate stoppage proneness in the industry, higher than in most of the 1950s and 1960s but lower than in the late 1940s and early 1950s. While there was considerable year to year variation over the decade, no trend is apparent in the data.

In sum, disputes on the New Zealand waterfront are comparatively frequent, moderate in scope but short in duration. Strikes, stop-work meetings, and bans predominate, arising most often over award claims, union business, demarcation, and social and political issues. Local port officials are the stoppage leaders and the pattern of disputes shows little trend over the last decade. This pattern is certainly not random and it is to an explanation of it that we now turn.

Interpreting the Pattern of Industrial Action

The market for shipping services is notoriously unstable: seasonal factors, the weather, the economy, and the scheduling of shipping companies all conspire to produce variation. Waterside work is only available when there is cargo to be handled, and seldom is the flow of cargo steady. The demand for labour can, therefore, oscillate wildly, and it is this variation that underlies much of the conflict in the industry. A regular employment relationship between a particular employer and worker has not developed on the waterfront. In the past, workers had to run the gauntlet of the 'auction block' system, where employers chose from the men seeking work on any day. The inequities and suspicion stemming from that system still influence the industry despite its change to a commission form of organisation forty years ago and despite the further step toward regular employment made in the 1970 award, which provided, at larger ports, for a guaranteed weekly wage equal to 40 hours at ordinary time rates.

The large number of employers at the bigger ports has compounded the problem. Employers appear very remote to the watersider who works for many different companies during the course of a year and whose only contact with them is the foreman stevedore supervising his work. On the waterfront, foremen are the focal point of management; they are under even greater pressure than in other industries. Not all of them stand up well to the strain. The merger process has in recent years led to a sharp reduction in the number of employers in the industry and this may lead to improved relations between employers and employees.

Shipping and stevedoring companies face other problems in forging a close relationship with waterside workers, not the least of which is their foreign ownership. In the minds of workers few employers have so sinister an aura surrounding them as overseas shipowners. Their organisation into conferences reinforces the view that waterside workers are confronting 'profiteering' international monopolists. Even the ownership ogre, however, may be fading with the formation of joint ventures between waterside workers' unions and shipping or stevedoring companies (Turkington, 1976: 274). The first of these ventures was established at the port of Mount Maunganui in 1975, and since then many others have followed. While it is easy to over-state both their importance and their influence on industrial relations, numerous observers in the industry hail these joint ventures as a major advance.

Opportunities for developing favourable relationships between employers and workers are much slimmer in this than in other industries. Few stable employment relationships exist; the watersider's most enduring relationship is with his port union. The peculiar employment situation on the waterfront has in the past led to many disputes and even today is conducive to industrial action. It means that watersiders and their employers are more willing, and in a sense more able, to engage in industrial action than their counterparts in other industries.

Some employers argue that the organisational structure of the industry, and particularly the Waterfront Industry Commission, leads to disputes. They would agree with the view that 'at the moment it is impossible to get worker loyalty to the employer. The Commission is a barrier which separates the two groups. The employers must become an identity [and] should run what they are paying for' (quoted in Turkington, 1976: 265). However, in view of the unstable demand for waterfront labour it is difficult to conceive of a viable alternative to the commission form of organisation. The WIC, in carrying out many tasks normally performed by employers, is seen by some of them as a barrier to closer relations with their employees. But by the same token, it is undoubtedly seen by workers as a buffer between them and employers whom they have historically regarded with great suspicion. The general view of workers is that 'the Commission has done away with many of the arguments and has led to harmony' (quoted in Turkington, 1976: 265).

The unusual employment relationship on the New Zealand waterfront has resulted in a uniquely homogeneous labour force. Admittedly, there are certain specialist positions, but these are available to any watersider with the necessary qualifications. Watersiders are rotated from one job to another and even from one area to another. They also work fairly equal hours so there is little differentiation among them in terms of occupation or income. Moreover, they are almost uniformly middle-aged and exclusively male. There is some racial diversity, with certain ports having a high proportion of Maoris, but overall the work force is predominantly white.

This homogeneous workforce is reflected in highly cohesive port unions that almost naturally conduct much of their business through stop-work meetings. Occasionally, the employer suffers as a result, but that is not likely to constrain watersiders unduly. Union strategies in the conduct of disputes, protests over employer actions, and internal union matters are typical of issues discussed at these meetings. Membership turnout is close to 100 per cent, partly because the workforce is so cohesive, especially when in dispute with the employer. Reinforcing this are the rules of many port unions that make it compulsory for members to attend authorised meetings or even unauthorised special meetings. Watersiders are almost habitual meeting attenders and will readily stop during working hours to discuss an issue. Indications are that their stop-work meetings are well organised and provide workers with an ample opportunity to air their opinions.

The homogeneity of the workforce and the lack of permanent work groups also help to explain the infrequency of sectional stoppages. Issues important to one group of workers are likely to be of concern to others and so to involve all watersiders at a port. The important role played by union officials in the conduct of disputes, together with the ready availability of the port conciliation committee, help prevent localised issues being manifested as sectional stoppages. Of those sectional stoppages that do occur, virtually none take place without the union's knowledge and blessing.

The cohesiveness of waterside workers places them in a strong organisational position to launch stoppages. These disputes might be expected to be especially vehement when they involve the encroachment of other workers on territory claimed by watersiders. Given their close proximity, it is not surprising that harbour board employees are occasionally seen to trespass and so to become opponents in demarcation disputes. This occasional conflict between the two groups is one of the elements that prevents them from combining in joint action against employers.

While watersiders jealously guard their work, they are far from parochial and traditionally have been in the forefront of the social and political activities of the New Zealand trade union movement. In dealing with international shipping they are almost inevitably confronted with a wider range of issues than the average trade unionist. Watersiders have thus stopped work on several occasions in protest at visits to New Zealand ports by nuclear warships and have placed bans on French, Chilean, and South African vessels in protest at the policies of those countries (Turkington, 1977a). As occupants of a strategic position in trade, water-siders are relied upon to spearhead many initiatives of the union move-ment. Not all their social and political concerns are international in character: waterside workers have staunchly supported protests over do-mestic policy, especially those involving economic questions such as inflation, incomes policy, and the like.

Watersiders gain bargaining power from their strategic position in domestic and international trade. When effectively harnessed through organisation, this power has been used to extract concessions from em-ployers and has been seen in the ability of watersiders to launch stoppages. The short duration of stoppages may reflect the tendency of employers to 'give in' when faced with worker pressure. Through their organisation into conferences, shipping companies effectively set their own freight rates and, as near-monopolists, are able to lead a quiet life by conceding when faced with a stoppage; cost increases are passed on in higher rates.

It is, however, easy to over-state the bargaining power of waterside workers by confusing the short with the long run. Employers are by no means loath to respond to worker pressure by diverting future shipping; this tactic, over the long run, eventually can undermine the bargaining power of workers. Watersiders at small and already declining ports have very little bargaining power indeed.

The nature of the work makes it peculiarly suited to the use of the ban as a form of industrial action. In the absence of employer retaliation, workers can impose a ban on a particular line, ship, container, or item of cargo without losing wages. The ban can be costly to the employer yet almost costless to the workers imposing it. Watersiders' unions make considerable use of bans, while employers naturally dislike this tactic intensely.

Ports are complex places, often catering for many different types of vessels and cargoes. Vessels may be coastal, international, conventional, container, or roll-on–roll-off, for example. Their cargoes range from bulk wheat through to dangerous chemicals. A complicated set of agreements and rules has been developed to regulate the waterfront. Larger ports may have fifteen or more different agreements, each of which has to be nego-tiated and is a potential source of conflict. As one union official has observed: 'We are down to the Plimsol with Agreements and adaptations to Agreements' (Hewitt, 1979: 23). Some of the agreements are detailed and quite complicated. The main award for the industry is much larger and more complex than awards in most other industries. Its schedule of allowances and special rates for particular cargoes alone covers eight pages and individually lists hundreds of different types of cargo. There is plenty of opportunity for continuing negotiation over such a complex document, which, despite the industry's system of dispute settlement, occasionally ends up in stoppages.

The waterside has traditionally been labour intensive but, in the space of a decade or so, considerable capital investment has taken place. Massive container and roll-on–roll-off terminals have been matched by dramatic increases in the cost and complexity of vessels.

Few industries have changed as rapidly as this one, and with the high rate of change has come conflict. The labour-replacing nature of the new technology is clear to workers, who have sought to safeguard their jobs. Employers have had to buy a reduction in the labour force through voluntary redundancy agreements. These agreements have helped check disputes over the pace at which the workforce is being reduced. Yet, while it fell by 20 per cent during the years 1972 to 1978, employers would like to see even fewer workers on the wharves. The scope for further voluntary redundancies, however, is now quite narrow, and disputes over the size of the labour force are far from over.

Conflict can also surround the making of agreements to cover the new technologies. Almost every new type of vessel has been greeted by disputes of one sort or another. The bans imposed, for example, on early container and lighter-aboard-ship vessels (ships that carry large barges that are loaded or unloaded at ports), have already been mentioned. Such bans were often introduced because agreements covering the new vessels had not been concluded.

New technologies also blur traditional occupational boundaries and so give rise to demarcation disputes. These disputes have been particularly associated with containerisation. In the early seventies there were many arguments between the waterside workers' unions and unions of storemen and packers over the packing and unpacking of less than containerload containers (that contain cargo from more than one consignor or consignee). These disputes led to a Royal Commission on Containers, which reported in 1972 (see Royal Commission of Inquiry, 1972). While a stable situation now exists where less than container load containers are packed or unpacked by watersiders at the terminal and full container load containers (with cargo from only one shipper) are handled by employees of the consignor or consignee, the underlying conflict is still simmering. Disagreements also arise between watersiders and employers over just what is a less than container load.

The relative frequency of demarcation disputes on the waterfront helps account for the low incidence of sympathy disputes observed in Table 4.4. Most of the unions that might seek sympathy support from waterside workers seldom ask for or get it because these very same unions are involved from time to time in demarcation disputes with watersiders.

The new equipment used in handling containers has itself led to many disputes. An example concerns union coverage of the 'transtainer' crane used to load and unload containers from railway wagons in the port of Wellington. Both railway workers and watersiders claimed coverage and after a long dispute the crane is now operated by the composite workforce of the container terminal, which largely consists of watersiders.

As they see employment opportunities declining, waterside workers have become even more vigilant in safeguarding work they consider to be theirs. A solution to the continual problem of demarcation may lie in the amalgamation of unions on the waterfront. This is occurring to a limited extent with the merger of shipwrights and tally clerks with watersiders. But amalgamation is a difficult and slow process. Talks about a possible merger have been held between the New Zealand Waterside Workers' Federation and the New Zealand Harbour Boards Employees' Union, but these petered out. There are many problems associated with such a merger. The Harbour Boards Employees' Union has a majority of members who are unconnected with cargo handling and who have no interest in joining with waterside workers. Watersiders, for their part, are interested mainly in the minority concerned with cargo handling. The differences in structure between the national union of harbour board employees and the port unions of watersiders further compound the problem. Many harbour board employees would argue that 'if watersiders can't amalgamate themselves, they will not do so with others'.

The declining numbers of watersiders have led their unions to push even harder for good wages and conditions. In the 1978 award they succeeded in gaining an undertaking that waterfront wages in the subsequent 1979 award would be set at the base rate for carpenters and related tradesmen in the building industry. While it can be argued that this is not a binding precedent for future awards, it will be treated as such by watersiders and can be regarded as quite an achievement for workers who have always been regarded as casual and unskilled.

The varying incidence of technological change helps explain why the larger ports are more prone to disputes than the smaller ones. Technological change has been most rapid at the large ports and has had the effect of diverting trade away from the small ones. Conventional cargo operations have remained the norm at small ports which, if anything, have fewer conflicts as they try desperately to retain trade (Turkington, 1976: 274–279).

What is surprising about the waterfront is not that disputes have arisen over technological change but that there have not been more of them. This may be partly due to the system of dispute settlement. The flexibility of the port conciliation committees sets them apart from dispute committees in other industries and helps ensure that disagreements are dealt with at source. Many disputes are settled at the ship's side within minutes of arising. As permanent bodies, the port committees are not only readily available but are also able to establish a high degree of credibility in the minds of the parties. There is widespread agreement in the industry that the port conciliation committees are both necessary and effective (Turkington, 1976: 267–269). The Waterfront Industry Tribunal has also been successful in resolving disputes, particularly those concerned with demarcation. Designed specifically for the waterfront, these bodies have been sufficiently flexible to survive the dramatic change occurring within the industry and, if anything, can be credited with facilitating it.

The high degree of organisation of both workers and employers in the industry is itself an important part of its accommodation structure. The officials of the NZWWF and the port unions on the one hand and of the NZWEU on the other, maintain close contact and sit together on many joint committees. While there is very little communication between worker and employer, this is partly compensated for by an unusually high degree of communication between officials of the representative organisations.

Conclusions

The pattern of disputes on the New Zealand waterfront is characterised by frequent but short stoppages involving quite large numbers of workers. Arising most often over award claims, union business, demarcation, and social and political issues, these disputes mainly take the form of the strike, stop-work meeting, or ban.

Underlying much of this industrial action is the irregular flow of shipping. In New Zealand the commission form of organisation and, as in some other countries, a type of permanent employment scheme has been developed to cope with this inherent problem. These efforts have met with some success, although the past still haunts the present and an established and committed relationship between worker and employer has never developed. The relatively high frequency of disputes on the waterfront reflects the comparative willingness of the parties to engage in action that is detrimental to the other's interests.

The homogeneity of waterside workers together with their union structure mean that the scope of disputes is broad. Sectional stoppages are rare in an industry where issues concern the whole labour force at the port and where union officials are the leaders in strike situations. These same features help also to explain the relatively frequent use of stop-work meetings.

The watersiders' location at the interface between the domestic economy and the world has given them an unusually wide perspective and the bargaining power with which to pursue a wide range of political and social issues. The power of watersiders, nevertheless, varies between ports, depending on the volume of trade, the employer's ability to divert trade in the future, and so on. This variation assists in explaining differences in dispute-proneness between the ports.

The waterfront industry has seen dramatic technological change, which has been greeted coolly by the workers it is intended to replace. While voluntary redundancy agreements have facilitated a decline in the labour force, further reductions are likely to give rise to disputes. Agreements covering the new technology have been difficult to make and have often only been concluded after the new technology has arrived. Relations among the unions connected with the waterfront have been worsened by technological change, and disputes between them have been common. Pressure to amalgamate has built up, but the process is slow and very far from complete. If anything, technological change has spurred watersiders on to push even harder for premium wages and conditions for those who remain. Large ports have seen much more technological change, and conflict resulting from it, than have small ones. Communications difficulties, variations in cargoes and conditions, complex agreements and rules, as well as the bargaining power already mentioned, are other features making large ports more prone to disputes.

The waterfront is increasingly moving in the direction of a skilled, capital intensive industry. Along the way there will continue to be disputes as the parties adjust to the changing situation. For unions used to separate identities and limited coverage this process of adjustment is difficult. Amalgamation, involving some smaller unions and waterside workers, is already underway and may broaden in scope, although the degree of compromise necessary among the larger unions will not come easily. Employers, for t'.eir part, are also having to adjust, sometimes by entering into joint ventures with local port unions. The representative character of the Waterfront Industry Commission should give it the flexibility and credibility to not only survive but also to assist the process of change. The dispute settlement bodies of the waterfront will also contribute to this process.

If disputes are not to escalate in the future, there is need for an even higher level of consultation and negotiation between the NZWEU and the NZWWF. Some of these consultations may have to involve other worker and employer organisations for the limits of waterfront work are becoming increasingly blurred. Co-ordination, planning and discussion are more necessary now than ever. But, however much the parties consult and negotiate, there is no guarantee that conflict will not arise. In this industry a certain measure of conflict is inevitable and even desirable.

NOTES

1. A full introduction to the New Zealand waterfront industry can be found in Turkington (1976: 223–232).
2. In the New Zealand Department of Statistics' industrial breakdown of disputes, harbour boards are reported as having experienced only fifteen stoppages over the decade 1969–78. While the usual problem of under-reporting of stoppages may affect this total, the 'harbour boards' classification covers all harbour board employees and not just the minority directly concerned with cargo handling.

CHAPTER FIVE

Bureaucracy, Job Control and Militancy:

The Case of Telecom Australia*

Barry Muller

In 1975 the Australian Post Office, a department of State, was divided into two statutory authorities: Australia Post and Telecom Australia. The latter organisation is entrusted with the supply of domestic telecommunications services. International services are provided by a separate statutory authority, while the manufacture of equipment used by these organisations is largely undertaken within the private sector.[1]

Telecom Australia has a number of distinguishing features that make it important. The functions of the organisation outlined in the Telecommunications Act, 1975 ensure that its activities pervade most aspects of Australian community life. Both business and the public are reliant on some service provided by Telecom, be it telephone, telegram, or telex services, the transmission of data, or radio or television broadcasts. Telecom's monopoly position conferred on it by the Act gives it a crucial role within industry and society generally.

In employment terms, Telecom is the largest enterprise in Australia.[2] Because of its possible influence on earnings relativities across a wide range of occupational groups, the National Government pays close attention to industrial relations in this organisation.

Since its formation, Telecom has experienced an increasing number of industrial relations problems, particularly involving technical workers. Similar behaviour amongst highly skilled work groups has been described in studies of the 'new working class' in other countries (Mallet, 1975;

*I would like to thank Telecom Australia for providing a scholarship, which enabled this study to be undertaken. Invaluable advice given by Stephen Frenkel is also much appreciated.

Low-Beer, 1978). The present investigation reveals a historical relationship between management and unions based on a dominant managerial philosophy and what is described as *dependent* behaviour by most trade unions. By contrast, the actions of one of the unions in rejecting the role cast for it by management has contributed to a new pattern of industrial action. The nature of this *independent* behaviour and the factors underlying its emergence form the major focus of this chapter.

The study is set in Queensland. It begins with a discussion of management and union organisation. In a subsequent section the patterns of conflict are described, and two distinct industrial action profiles are identified. The third section discusses the characteristics of accommodation between management and unions, focusing especially on the changing attitudes of the workers and the corresponding alterations and continuities in management and union behaviour.

Structure and Goals

The structure of the enterprise is at once bureaucratic and highly centralised. Functional control is delegated to various groups within a national administration. They are responsible for the co-ordination of planning and the formulation of policy with regard to the organisation's operations, structure, and workforce. Each of the six states, including Queensland, has its own administration responsible for the exercise of line control, interpretation and application of policy, as well as the collection of data for the national planning process. Customer services are provided by a number of district sub-structures within each state.

A separate industrial relations function was created in 1969 following a period of industrial turbulence in the latter half of the sixties. Within the national administration it has a policy-making role, including responsibility for negotiations with the national bodies of the unions and representation at the AC&AC. It is equivalent to other functional areas and provides advice to senior management at a national level. Within the State administrations, the industrial relations function is one of interpretation of policy and negotiation with the State branches of the unions on local issues.

In 1975 the nature of the industrial relations role within the organisation was changed. The determination of pay and conditions of employment prior to that had resided with the Public Service Board.[3] Since then Telecom management has acquired these functions although its discretion is circumscribed by the National Government. A co-ordination committee consisting of representatives from the Public Service Board and the Government's Industrial Relations Department determines Telecom's response to union claims and the acceptability of management's initiatives conce; ning pay and conditions of employment. This is the major means by wh'ch the Government influences the industrial relations policy of the enterprise, although it does have some say in strategies adopted in disputes through the advisory role of its Industrial Relations Department.

Since its inception in 1975, Telecom has adopted a modern, aggressive marketing approach to its operations. Emphasis has increasingly been placed on satisfying consumer demand and minimising price increases. Unlike its predecessor, and most other statutory authorities, at least half of Telecom's capital expenditure must be financed internally while the balance of investment funds is obtained on the semi-government loans market. These new marketing and financial objectives have led to top management adopting a particularly cost conscious approach to business operations. Since labour constitutes 45 per cent of annual expenditure, it is an obvious target for cost savings. This is demonstrated by the drastic curtailment of increases in the size of the workforce, despite abnormally high growth in demand for services over recent years. Stabilisation of employment levels has been facilitated by the introduction of new technology, which has also contributed to increased labour productivity in recent years.[4]

Management has become strongly committed to centralised planning as a vehicle for the achievement of its goals. Planning embraces all levels of the workforce and determines workload, pace of work, the type and amount of equipment used and conditions under which work is performed. While planning has always played a major role in the operation of the organisation, in more recent years control has intensified through a growing standardisation and formalisation of management processes.[5] This is suggested by the following extract from the 1977–78 Annual Report:

> The drive to contain capital investments was continued through close senior management attention to projects and programmes, by setting demanding targets at many levels throughout the organisation and closely monitoring the results, by the development of comprehensive programming and planning and by the careful exploitation of new technologies in many areas of Telecom's activities. (Telecom Australia Annual Report 1977–78, p.12)

Technological change is rapidly becoming the chief means of improving productivity and increasing consumer demand for communication services. Current plans indicate that changes in the near future will be massive by comparison with the past.[6] Naturally, the implications for the workforce and the unions are the subject of much controversy.

The workers referred to in this chapter are allocated to one of four

TABLE 5.1

Union size and coverage in Telecom Queensland, 1978

Name	Abbreviated designation	Skill group covered	Size in Telecom Queensland	Percentage of total membership in Queensland
Australian Telecommunications Employees Association	ATEA	Technical	3593	100
Australian Postal & Telecommunications Union	APTU	Lines	4300	60
Administrative & Clerical Officers Association	ACOA	Clerical	1038	20
Australian Public Service Association (4th division officers)	APSA	Clerical	602	20
Australian Telephonist & Phonogram Officers Association	ATPOA	Operator	1640	100
Union of Postal Clerks and Telegraphists	UPCT	Operator	69	9

Source: Trade union records.

major skill groups; technical, lines, clerical, and operator, comprising 80 per cent of the workforce. *Technical* workers are responsible for the installation and maintenance of the communications network while *lines* workers are employed in installing the connections between telephone exchanges and subscribers. The *clerical* group are responsible for administrative tasks and the *operator* group provide telephone and telegraphic services. A substantial majority of these four groups of workers are organised by six unions. Membership units tend to coincide with the skill groups, so that reference to any one of them can be regarded as reference also to the specific unions (see Table 5.1).

Trade unionism has existed for many years in the organisation, including its predecessor. It has been encouraged by the conciliation and arbitration system. Indeed, many of the twenty-four unions that represent the total Telecom workforce could not have continued to this day were it not for the jurisdictional legal protection afforded by the accommodation system.
Service; its major features continue to persist in Telecom. These are: high membership density, which includes supervisory staff; full-time union officials drawn from the workforce, yet remaining on long term leave; provision of union facilities such as check-off; the opportunity to attend union meetings at the workplace; and trade union training courses without loss of pay.

Over the past five years the Queensland State branches of the main unions have taken a number of steps to improve their organisational effectiveness. Among the most far reaching of these steps have been the increasing number of full-time officials provided by changes in union rules; encouragement given by the officials to lay activists to attend government sponsored trade union training courses; and organisational restructuring by the ATEA following leadership changes in a number of State branches in the early 1970s.

The recruitment and mobilisation of members is carried out at the State branch level, but the responsibility for policy-making and negotiations on the substantive rules lies with Federal union executives. These consist of national full-time officials and representatives of the State branches. In short, union structure tends to parallel that of Telecom, with centralisation being a common denominator.

By contrast, the ATEA differs from the other unions. Its rules require that all policy must either originate with the rank and file or be ratified at meetings of the members. It is customary for important decisions to be taken at mass meetings. It is evident that the ATEA places a good deal of emphasis on membership participation and the decentralisation of authority.[7]

Most of the unions have workplace sub-structures whose effectiveness has only developed over the past five years. Here again, the ATEA is different. Whereas the other unions have formed shop steward organisations, the ATEA has developed a system of properly constituted sub-branches in most work areas. These units have greater autonomy than do the shop stewards of other unions.

Industrial Conflict: New Forms of Opposition

While strikes do occur in Telecom, they are much less common than black bans. Nevertheless, it is important to assess their relative importance in comparison with Telecom Australia-wide and Australian industry overall. This is made possible by data presented in Table 5.2

TABLE 5.2

Average number of working days 'lost' per 1000 workers, Telecom and Australia 1976–78*

	1976	1977	1978
Telecom Queensland	449	75	463
Australia	375	47	165
Australia (all industries)	770	335	430

*excludes bans.

Source: ABS, *Industrial Disputes*, Catalogue no. 6322.0 and Telecom Australia records.

It appears that Telecom in Queensland is substantially more strike-prone than is the organisation nationally.[8] But the data also suggest that, compared with the all-industry average, Telecom in Queensland is relatively free from industrial disputes.

In fact, analysis of Telecom Australia records for Queensland shows that in the period 1975–78, 78 per cent of working days 'lost' (again excluding bans) were attributable to stoppages of one day's duration or less. Furthermore, 38 per cent of these were stop-work meetings. These are a form of protest action and an indication of the level of support for an issue to union officials and management alike. They also allow members to voice their opinions and vote on strategy proposals. Since these meetings often take place in lunch braks, they are more prevalent than is indicated in the statistics.

Although work stoppages are infrequent, since 1975 their severity has been increasing. This is contrary to the national strike trend (ABS Catalogue no.6322.0: 1978). Table 5.3 provides some indication of this apparent upsurge in militancy.

The frequency of stoppages has not grown appreciably, but the number of workers involved has increased dramatically. Taken in conjunction

TABLE 5.3

*Characteristics of stoppages in Telecom Queensland in
selected periods*

	1971–74	1975–78
Number of stoppages	11	13
Workers involved	1904	16 189
Working days 'lost'	877	14 295

Source: Telecom Australia internal records.

with the data in Table 5.3, the massive rise in working days 'lost' suggests that stoppages have also increased in duration.

Despite these indicators of a worsening industrial relations climate in Telecom, the strike remains a relatively rare industrial tactic. Bans have proved much more popular with the unions. In the period 1975–78 there were sixty-three disputes involving bans, compared with only thirteen that resulted in a work stoppage. By 1973 bans had become sufficiently important for Telecom to begin collecting data on this activity. Taking bans into account, the picture of Telecom (Queensland) as a relatively dispute-free organisation is reversed. Between 1975 and 1978 there has been an average of twenty disputes a year involving some form of industrial action, typically black bans. On the basis of data covering the period May 1975 to the end of 1978, bans averaged slightly over ten weeks in duration. Indeed, there was no time during that period when at least one ban was not in force.

A ban is a refusal by workers to carry out some aspect of their job. It is a partial, as opposed to a complete, withdrawal of labour. From the standpoint of workers and unions, the advantage of the ban is that it enables other work to continue and hence wages to be paid. Furthermore, because bans are used selectively, they do not require a high level of commitment to industrial action by the majority of union members. Recent legislation (referred to in more detail on p.115) has been enacted in order to minimise this form of action. Nevertheless, during the period of this study, management was considerably inconvenienced, since the applications of bans are not offset by a lower wages bill.

Certain kinds of work are more conducive to the use of bans. Where tasks are sub-divided, but not interrelated (in the sense that one task cannot be undertaken without the other having been completed), bans are especially effective. In these cases bans may be applied without substantially disrupting the normal work routine. They may thus be used more readily as a means of pushing forward the workers' frontier of control and accordingly can be viewed as instruments of *aggression*. Where the work process is highly integrated, and the effect of a ban would be similar to a strike, bans are used less readily, usually in *defence* of workers' interests. These protest actions may, for example, signal disenchantment with safety standards, or some other aspect of working conditions, pace of work, or changes in work procedures.

It is not possible to quantify information on bans in the conventional sense as there is normally no time 'lost', and it is difficult to gauge the number of workers involved. The major issues precipitating industrial action are reflected in disputes resulting in bans rather than stoppages as Table 5.4 indicates.

TABLE 5.4

Number of stoppages and bans in Telecom Queensland, 1975–78, by cited issue

Cited Issue	Stoppages	Bans
Wages	1	1
Hours of work	3	2
Leave, pensions, compensation provisions etc.	1	4
Managerial policy and behaviour	5	44
Physical working conditions	1	7
Trade unionism	–	2
Political	2	–
Other	–	3
Total	13	63

Source: Telecom Australia internal records.

Managerial policy was cited as an issue in 70 per cent of disputes involving bans but in less than half of those involving stoppages. However, working days 'lost' over managerial policy and behaviour has been increasing: in 1971–74 just over 2 per cent of days 'lost' were occasioned by disputes in this category, in 1975–78 it had increased to 27 per cent.

Another feature of the conflict pattern concerns the location of industrial action at the national and State levels. State issues more commonly resulted in bans: forty-four bans and three strikes in the period were concerned with regional issues. This suggests that bans are more characteristic of industrial action at the State rather than the national level. Industrial action is also more prevalent at State level.[9]

Not all unions are equally disposed to engage in industrial action. Table

5.5 indicates that a large proportion of stoppages and bans are attributable to the ATEA.

TABLE 5.5

Number of stoppages and bans in Telecom Queensland, 1975–78 by union

Union	Stoppages %	Bans %	Employees in respective skill groups %
ATEA	42	54	31
Others	58	46	69
Total	100	100	100
Number of disputes and employees	19	63	12 189

Source: Telecom Australia internal records.

Of the remaining unions the APTU and the UPCT were involved in approximately 30 per cent of both forms of action. Additionally, the ATEA was responsible for almost 60 per cent of working days 'lost', which included the majority of stoppages lasting more than one day. It was also involved in half of the disputes concerning managerial policy and behaviour.

The ATEA has increasingly engaged in industrial disputation. In the period 1970–74 the ATEA was involved in 31 per cent of stoppages and was responsible for 19 per cent of working days 'lost'. During 1975–78 these figures increased to 42 per cent and 58 per cent respectively. The ATEA is also more likely to take part in stoppages of over one day's duration. Moreover, this union, almost alone, has employed bans as aggressive, tactical instruments: eleven of the thirty-four bans applied by ATEA members could be so categorised.

From the data presented above, two distinct profiles can be distinguished. One is characterised by a greater readiness to use industrial action of a more aggressive and prolonged nature, and it is more likely to arise from issues involving managerial actions. This is a pattern typified by the ATEA's activities. The converse of this, a relatively low propensity to resort to industrial action, use of the one day protest stoppage, and defensive rather than aggressive type bans, characterises the actions of the remaining unions.

Common features of both profiles are the extensive use of bans, a high percentage of short duration stoppages, disputes predominantly precipitated by managerial policy and behaviour, and an overall increase in industrial action since 1975.

Organisational Change and Industrial Action

The following discussion centres on the response of management, workers, and union officials to organisational change. While the attitudes of workers have altered, particularly within the technical group, management and union officials, with the exception of the ATEA, have continued to accommodate their interests in the traditional manner. The ATEA, on the other hand, is using a newly acquired realisation of its power to forge a different relationship with management.

An understanding of the conflict profiles is enhanced by an awareness of the perspectives management and union officials bring to industrial relations. Their respective ideologies determine some of the main organisational characteristics and strategies employed in industrial relations. Historical and environmental factors have combined to produce a managerial ideology that emphasises the unilateral authority of management in all but a few areas of management-worker relations. Certain expectations of trade union behaviour embodied in this philosophy have given rise to a dependence on management on the part of most unions. The rejection of this relationship by the ATEA marks the emergence of a more forthright, independent stance.

Management Ideology, Organisation, and Practice

Centralisation of decision-making within the enterprise has been accompanied by standardisation and formalisation of management processes. Senior management's aggressive pursuit of new goals consistent with its marketing orientation has resulted in an intensification of these management characteristics. The development of the planning process and the adoption of targets designed to reduce costs and improve efficiency have increased senior management's control of lower levels of the organisation.

Simultaneously, workers have been asked to co-operate in the attainment of these goals by raising their work effort and accepting rationalisation of work processes. Workers are required to accept increased work loads, less discretion, lower employment levels, and technological change. Great reliance is thus placed on management's attempts to obtain co-operation from the workforce. Indeed, as in the past, management have tried persistently to integrate workers into the organisation.

For example, workers enjoy security of employment, there are no arbitrary dismissals, and there are specified, complex procedures for terminating employment. Specialist training is required for a large percentage of the workforce because of the unique nature of tasks and the technology associated with telecommunications. Training is provided internally. Although for some workers skills are common to those of outside industry, for most their ability to use them outside Telecom is limited. The concept of lifetime career is encouraged by graduated promotion and skill structures and generous superannuation benefits. In June 1978, 51 per cent of the workforce had been employed in the organisation for ten years or more. Integration is seen to promote employee motivation and identification with the enterprise.

Prior to 1975, and under the aegis of the Public Service Board, the organisation and the unions were insulated from industrial relations in the private sector. The role of the Board in the formulation of industrial relations policy promoted collaboration between management and union officials in satisfying their mutual interests. Both acknowledged that the enterprise, as a public service, had certain responsibilities towards the general community and to its employees.

These attitudes facilitated industrial peace, but they militated against the achievement of market and efficiency goals. Management's views are grounded in a particular philosophy of organisational relationships, which has had, and continues to have, a profound effect on industrial relations. The term 'mutual interests philosophy' has been coined to summarise the essential features of this ideology. According to the mutual interests philosophy, the joint interests of both management and workers are served by the attainment of the organisation's objectives. Team work is of the essence, as the following passage from a key official document suggests: 'Within Telecom Australia there is widespread recognition of the loyalty of staff and their identification with the interests of the organisation' (Telecom Australia Corporate Plan, 1977: 10). To this extent, it is reminiscent of the Human Relations School of thought, particularly popular in the United States in the 1940s and 1950s.[10] It is, however, more a home-grown philosophy developing out of certain historical and environmental factors than any conscious strategy based on social science.[11]

Adherents to the mutual interests philosophy perceive conflict as a form of deviancy from normal functioning. It is assessed in accordance with its adverse effects on the enterprise. Again this is demonstrated in the Corporate Plan: 'it must be acknowledged that there are breakdowns in communications and relationships resulting in contention, loss of efficiency and disruption of work' (Telecom Australia Corporate Plan, 1977: 10).

The expression of conflict is regarded as unnecessary because management take it upon themselves to define what is in the best interests of their staff. This includes aspects of the work environment such as safety, working conditions, and welfare facilities and are explicitly taken into account in management decision-making. While 'good' industrial relations are not assumed by this philosophy, neither are they viewed as being especially problematic. The formula for obtaining the desired employee attitudes is an 'informed organisation' as is prescribed in the major planning document: 'For a properly motivated organisation of high morale and purpose, it is essential that management and staff at all levels be adequately informed and have effective systems of communications.' (Telecom Australia Implementation of the Corporate Plan, 1977: 34)

Implicit in a 'properly motivated organisation' is a high degree of co-operation from workers and their identification with management goals. As long as this can be achieved, supposedly by the injection of information and backed up by 'good' communications with workers, industrial relations will be accorded low priority. In interviews, industrial relations specialists at both national and State levels were of the opinion that they did not have sufficient influence with senior management, although this influence was considered to have increased with the recent upsurge in industrial action.

The policy of effective communications had its most liberal expression in a brief flirtation with consultative groups. These were formed in specific circumstances, mainly where organisational change was envisaged. These sub-structures, however, were not adopted as a permanent feature of organisational life. In any case, they did nothing to alter the distribution of power between management and workers.

The emphasis on communications, from the top of the organisation downwards, rather than a two-way process, is evident from the following extract taken from an address by a senior manager:

> Despite the many information bulletins and staff letters that have been issued and the many hours that have been spent by senior headquarters officers in discussions and explanations with ATEA officials, we have obviously failed to establish a full understanding of our objectives in the workplace. It is here that each of you have an important role to play by explaining to staff face to face the position of management in these issues, remembering that you yourselves are senior members of the management team and that it is your responsibility to know the facts and explain them to staff members who look to you for leadership. (Address to FYEOP Conference 1978)

This management approach assumes that worker identification with the goals of the organisation is a realistic aim. It also amounts to a refusal to acknowledge that the interest of workers and management may diverge substantially. Where more information and greater communication meet with failure, management resort to the use of overt power. Retaliatory action was taken against the ATEA in 1978 and again in 1979. This took the form of denying workers their pay while bans were imposed.

Management power has been bolstered by the introduction of legislation (Commonwealth Employees [Employment provision] Act, 1977), which permits workers to be arbitrarily layed off if they are affected by, or involved in, industrial action. In addition, the employment of those taking industrial action may be terminated. The Act, which is aimed specifically at bans, has already been applied to ATEA members during a dispute in mid 1979.

One of the main characteristics of the Act is that it empowers the relevant Minister to direct the application of sanctions, thereby appearing to involve the national government in the conduct of disputes. This has intensified industrial conflict and further undermined union confidence in the government and its procedural rules. Top management has meanwhile coupled a strategy of communication with an emphasis on legal sanctions against recalcitrant unions. Within Queensland, accommodation is being attempted through efforts to improve relationships with shop floor representatives and full-time union officials at the regional level.

However, the ATEA officials have spurned these contacts preferring to grant greater autonomy to their workplace representatives. In this way the representatives are given the opportunity to build relationships with line managers while the officials contribute to negotiations with Telecom industrial relations managers. Discordance in procedural preferences is manifested in the lack of management control over ATEA shop floor organisation and hence its higher propensity to engage in industrial action. Higher management has responded by further formalisation and centralisation of industrial relations in relation to the ATEA. It is noteworthy that in interviews with line managers at the State level there was a widespread desire to prevent industrial relations problems from escalating into senior management circles. Rules were interpreted broadly and even occasionally ignored in order to resolve issues promptly. But with the increasing centralisation and control of senior management over their lower order colleagues, such practices have become more difficult to sustain. Informal strategies are, therefore, rendered less effective; they nevertheless continue as one type of response to the growing centralisation, formalisation, and standardisation of management procedures.

Given management's approach to industrial relations, what role is there for the trade unions? In short, very little. They are granted recognition by management more as a consequence of the conciliation and arbitration system than as true representatives of workers' interests. The unions are not seen as independent sources of legitimate authority, they are rather expected to act as welfare appendages to the business enterprise. They are seen to have a residual function in bringing to management's attention matters that have been overlooked in the decision-making process. Trade unions are not accorded any rights in that process.

Union Ideology, Organisation and Strategies

Unions may be categorised according to their acceptance or rejection of management's definition of their role. Dependent unions are those (all but the ATEA) that comply with management's expectations. The goals of these unions are narrow, typically those that management are prepared to regard as legitimate. These unions are moderate in political outlook and rely on negotiations and ultimately arbitration to obtain their demands. They tend to be highly centralised, with little emphasis placed on rank and file participation. Militant tendencies among the membership are discouraged. When industrial action does take place it normally takes the form of a defensive ban or a short protest stoppage. This type of union behaviour may be termed the dependent action profile.

A union that is not prepared to accept the constraints placed upon it by the management necessarily becomes less reliant on the 'good faith' of management. This has been characteristic of the ATEA's behaviour in recent years. The ATEA leadership considers that many of its problems extend beyond the employer–employee relationship and include social and political policies that affect all workers and the community. Consequently, the union seeks a greater voice in the trade union movement. It is in this context that the union's relationship with management must be viewed. The union rejects management's definition of the interests of 'staff' and instead demands an equal say in decision-making. The central issues lie beyond the jurisdiction of the AC&AC and the Commission is seen by union officials as a tool of the employer. A structure facilitating rank and file participation in decision-making has been adopted, and local autonomy has been encouraged. The union's independence from management and its greater reliance on industrial action of a more aggressive kind can be described as the independent action profile. This pattern is a consequence of the attempt by the union to reach a new *modus vivendi* with management.

The relationship between the two types of unions (independent and dependent) and their respective industrial action profiles requires explanation. Our argument will focus on differences in member attitudes and union power resources as the key elements that distinguish these types of unions and their industrial action patterns. The Telecom organisation can be described as bureaucratic or mechanistic (Burns and Stalker, 1961). Its characteristics have been associated with high levels of dissatisfaction (Argyris, 1964) and low trust relations (Fox, 1974). While generalised low trust can be shown to apply to management–worker relationships in

Telecom, this does not explain differences in the industrial action profiles. The greater readiness of technical workers to resort to industrial action is, however, understandable by reference to the impact of increasing standardisation and formalisation of management procedures[12] on workers performing traditionally high discretion work roles (Low-Beer, 1978). In addition, a militant response is evoked by the strategies and style of unions who are more concerned to mobilise, rather than suppress, workers' discontent.

Low Trust and Discontent

A relatively high degree of standardisation and formalisation of management processes has always been characteristic of this public enterprise. However, these increased in the early 1970s with the development of centralised planning in the technical and lines area. The drive for greater productivity reached a peak after 1975 with the increased centralisation of management control systems relating to all skill groups.

The planning process and efforts to meet production targets have tended to restrict line management's flexibility to respond to workers' desires. This bureaucratic standardisation of management behaviour led many workers to the view that management had little regard or respect for them. This was reciprocated by workers in terms of a decline in trust. For example: 'management tells us half-truths and always interprets regulations in their favour', and 'with the lies emanating from top management Telecom cannot be trusted.'

Management's lack of credibility was highlighted during recent disputes with the ATEA: notices sent to technical workers were often returned to management unopened. In one particular dispute with the same union a profusion of literature was accompanied by management attempts to withhold the pay of workers who refused to carry out all the designated functions of their job. Not surprisingly, low trust relations have become endemic amongst the technicians. Moreover, management's low level of legitimacy has been further eroded by recent attempts to introduce new technology. The unions have made much of management's refusals to provide adequate information and to negotiate at an early stage.

Job security becomes important to workers in an environment of rapid technological change (see Table 5.9). Interviews with shop floor representatives and union officials revealed that security of employment was seen by them as one of the major issues of the future and one likely to attract a high level of support from the members. This is not surprising given the new work effort norms currently being established. Any sudden downturn in demand occasioned by a rise in prices or saturation of the market for new telephone services would highlight excess labour resources. The fear of unemployment and the lack of unqualified assurances to relieve such doubts have served to reinforce feelings of insecurity and low trust.

To make matters worse, recent legislation[13] has been interpreted by the unions as a method of reducing public sector employment where redundancies occur. Although Telecom management has indicated it will not use the legislation, this did not prevent participation of approximately 360 ACOA members and 28 lower management personnel in a one day stoppage in mid 1979. This was called in order to seek the withdrawal of the legislation. It is worth noting that a stoppage of this size by clerical workers is unprecedented amongst Telecom's Queensland members.

Low trust implies that workers will not readily accept management's right to make decisions. The extent of management decision-making legitimacy is reported in Table 5.6.

TABLE 5.6

*Workers' acceptance of management's decisions by skill group**

	Technical group %		Other groups %	
Employees are obliged to follow management's instructions because:				
(a) They are the experts	1		7	
(b) It is an obligation under the work contract	30		38	
		31		45
Employees should not necessarily or automatically follow management's instructions because:				
(a) They are not always right	46		43	
(b) They do not take account of employees' interests	23		12	
		69		55
Total		100		100
Number of respondents		95		136

*Significant at the 0.05 level using the chi-square test.
Source: Workforce Survey.[14]

The table shows that technicians are more likely to challenge management's decision-making powers (69 per cent) than other workers (55 per cent); in both cases largely on the grounds of possible incompetence. ATEA members also tend to reject management's decisions on the grounds that they do not take account of employees' interests (23 per cent). Both sets of workers, nevertheless, show that they are poorly integrated into the organisation. In particular, the technicians are likely to challenge management's decisions and demand a greater degree of job control. This issue is discussed later in connection with workers' grievances (p.123).

If low trust is a general response by workers in Telecom to developments in management policy, this by itself does not explain the relative militancy of the technical workers. The sources of their discontent require an appreciation of changes in their work tasks.

With the introduction of new generation telecommunications technology during the 1960s and early 1970s the skills of the technical groups were elevated from mechanic level to those of fully certified technicians requiring sub-professional qualifications. The following partial job description gives some idea of the qualities required: 'it includes the analysis of the most complex system faults usually in critical situations or where high level diagnostic skill is required.' (Australian Public Service Position Classification Standards)

The traditional work of the technician also allows considerable autonomy since tasks are carried out individually or in small groups with a minimum of supervision. The work of other skill groups contrasts with that of the technicians. Telephonists, telegraphists, and clerical workers are largely involved in low discretion, routine tasks performed in large groups under supervisory control. Linesmen work in gangs and have greater task discretion, but close supervision is nevertheless fairly common.

The significant point appears to be that the technical group experiences the structure of the organisation and the limitations placed on discretion differently to the other groups. This is borne out by the results of a survey question that asked respondents to indicate their awareness of the centralised nature of the organisation and the constraints imposed by the standardisation and formalisation of management processes. Table 5.7 provides the relevant data.

The technicians appear to lament the fact that they are excluded from the centralised decision-making process (73 per cent). But alienation is also evident among the other skill groups (49 per cent). Discontent with the decision-making process is supported by two other sets of data. A prior study of the relationship between management and technical workers showed that, in the opinion of most workers, management withheld information, communicated work directives without adequate explanation, and failed to seek the views of workers on how particular tasks could be best performed. (Jansen, Thompson, Zantis, 1978)

The second piece of evidence comes from a management initiated

TABLE 5.7

Workers' perceptions of the organisation's structure by skill group*

Statements	Technical group %	Other groups %
Most of the decisions that affect the employee are made at the top and the employee has no contact with top management	73	49
While some of the decisions are made at the top, the employee can contact the relevant management on many matters of importance to him.	27	51
Total	100	100
Number of respondents	95	136

*Significant at the 0.001 level using the chi-square test.
Source: Workforce Survey.

report into problems associated with the technicians in 1975 (Review Team 2, 1975). The following observation was made by the researchers: 'many times in our interviews staff (technicians and telecommunications assistants) stated that they had been forced to work within forms of organisation "imposed from on high" with no advice or discussion with those involved' (p.18). The report noted that lack of involvement in decision-making was a major source of dissatisfaction. This, and other pieces of evidence, suggest that the technicians view work, and the organisation in which tasks are executed, as a central life interest (Dubin, 1956). While the ATEA had reorganised its structure to facilitate the demands by technicians for participation in union affairs, the same cannot be said of Telecom. Increasingly, union demands are taking the form of claims for involvement in decision-making on managerial issues. Examples include finance, manpower, marketing, the organisation structure of the enterprise, and, most importantly, the introduction of new technology.

Management has attempted to alleviate discontent over the possible implications of technological change by undertaking not to use recent legislation specifically catering for redundancy. A clause has also been inserted in the technicians' award to the effect that there will be no redundancies due to technological change for ten years. These positive steps have been treated with scepticism by the unions. This is largely because major decisions affecting technology and organisational structure have been determined unilaterally by senior management.

Finally, in connection with the dissatisfaction felt by technicians, mention must be made of declining promotion opportunities. Promotion is one of the most important job priorities of these workers (Table 5.9) yet education barriers that violate career expectations have been introduced into promotion and skill structures of the technical and lines groups. Moreover, in the case of the technicians, 60 per cent of the supervisors are below forty years of age, limiting promotion chances even further.

It should be clear from the above discussion that technicians are particularly disenchanted with their work role, but does this imply a higher degree of conflict consciousness?

An awareness of a divergence of interests between workers and management has emerged amongst employees in all occupational groups. Typical interview comments include the following:

> Telecom appears to place more value on the 'almighty dollar' than the individual.

> Management seem to push production too much, hence avoiding safety issues.

> Money and targets have become the number one goal without full consideration of human satisfaction in the job.

The subordination of social goals to economic efficiency is a frequent critical theme, but the extent to which awareness of conflicting interests varies between occupation groups is particularly clear from data presented in Table 5.8. The data indicate that technicians are considerably more inclined than other workers to believe that industrial action is often the only way to get consideration of employee interests (79 per cent). This constitutes a significant refutation of a central tenet of the mutual interests philosophy.

Union Responses to Low Trust and Workers' Discontent

It is now necessary to discuss the differences between the dependent and independent union strategies in order to illustrate our argument that the ATEA represents a new form of unionism within the industry. Firstly, we must ask whether the goals of these two types of unions reflect differences in the priorities and problems faced by their respective members. Table 5.9 reports the factors considered by workers to be most important in making a job worthwhile.

With the exception of a greater emphasis placed on promotion by the technical group, and a stronger preference for congenial workmates by the other groups, there are no important differences between the priorities

TABLE 5.8

*Workers' perceptions of management's concern for their
interests by skill group**

Statement	Technical group %	Other groups %
Management usually takes into account the interests of its employees in its decision making	21	57
Industrial action is often the only way to get consideration of employees' interests	79	43
Total	100	100
Number of respondents	95	136

*Significant at the 0.001 level using the chi-square test.
Source: Workforce Survey.

TABLE 5.9

Workers' assessment of important job factors by skill group

Factor	Technical group % *	Other groups % *
Security	60	66
Good money	59	49
Interesting work	55	49
Fair management	27	25
Good working conditions	27	26
Good promotion prospects	35	21
Good workmates	10	25
Responsibility	13	9
A strong union	5	9
Easy atmosphere	6	6
Number of respondents	95	136

*Columns do not add to 100 because each worker was asked to nominate three choices. The numbers represent the percentage of workers who chose each factor.
Source: Workforce Survey.

of the two sets of workers. Overall, security of employment, good money, interesting work, good working conditions, and fair management are the most valued aspects of work.

To what extent were management meeting these aspirations? Although there is no direct evidence from the workforce survey, an analysis of grievances provided by eleven and thirty-two workplace representatives from the ATEA and other unions respectively is highly revealing. Table 5.10 presents a summary of this information.

While the majority of job grievances reported by non-ATEA job delegates centre upon wages, employment and working conditions, safety, and shiftwork, those of the ATEA focus a good deal on work allocation and task performance, with safety coming a very poor second. Furthermore, the number of grievances per ATEA job delegate (three) is considerably higher than among their other union counterparts (two). Discontent amongst the ATEA members appears to be more common and to focus much more on management. This suggests that low trust is particularly characteristic of relationships between ATEA members and management.

TABLE 5.10

*Grievances reported by job delegates over the most recent three months**

Type of grievance	ATEA %	Other unions %
Work allocation and task performance	44	11
Pay and conditions of employment	9	18
Working conditions	6	11
Safety	18	22
Shiftwork	3	12
Complaints regarding supervision	6	8
Discrimination	11	10
Other	3	8
Total	100	100
Number of grievances	34	73

*Interviews were conducted in the period March to June 1979
Source: job delegate interviews.

How have the unions responded to their members' problems? The officials from the dependent unions have continued in the customary way: pursuing grievances through negotiations with management and a reliance on arbitration. This is facilitated by the nature of the members' grievances, which, in contrast to many of those pursued by the ATEA, are viewed by management as legitimate issues for joint or third party resolution.

The ATEA, which represents the independent style of union behaviour, has, as noted in a previous section, resorted to industrial action to a much greater extent than the other unions. This can be accounted for by the union's reaction to the specific type of grievances articulated by the members.

Technical workers have been increasingly subject to greater management control in the exercise of their work tasks. In addition, reduction in employment levels relative to demand, unilaterally decided upon and executed by management in accordance with their drive for greater efficiency, are manifested in the large number of work allocation and task performance grievances. The important point here is that these are defined by management and tribunals alike as issues that lie outside the area of joint regulation or arbitration.[15] Faced with refusals by management to negotiate, and with no recourse to arbitration (since the law upholds management prerogatives), the ATEA has adopted a militant approach to industrial relations. The members have responded positively, their feelings being grounded in a sense of moral outrage against attempts to rationalise and hence reduce those factors that are most valued by these workers (see Table 5.9).

The ATEA officials have been able to further promote and organise discontent by focusing the members' attention on the issue of technological change. The introduction of new technology has been relatively minor since 1975 compared to what is being planned by management for the future. Massive changes are expected to affect most skill groups, yet it appears that only the ATEA have been able to mobilise their members' discontent around this issue. Indeed, that the other unions have paid little attention to it is partly reflected in the data reported in Table 5.11.

The technical workers appear much more apprehensive about the effects of new technology than their counterparts in the other occupational groups, in spite of the fact that technological change to date has not been any more common in the technical than in the other work areas. Discontent has, nevertheless, been sufficiently strong to enable the ATEA to undertake large national campaigns involving industrial action in 1977 and 1978.

The initial technology dispute in 1977 served to alert officials to the need for greater solidarity amongst members on this issue. A lengthy campaign followed. Union members and the public were educated on the problems of technology. The 1978 dispute of four weeks duration resulted in major disruption to the network, during which over 4000 workers had their pay withheld for participating in bans.[16]

The ATEA is a left wing union: the leadership refuses to accept a

TABLE 5.11

*Workers' assessment of the effect of technological change
on their jobs by skill group**

Workers assessment	Technical group %	Other groups %
Favourable	13	42
Unfavourable	73	29
No effect	14	29
Total	100	100
Number of respondents	95	136

*Significant at the 0.001 level using the chi-square test.
Respondents were asked the following question: Telecom has introduced, or is in the process of introducing, changes in its technology. What effect, if any, do you think these changes have had, or will have on the important aspects of your job?

Source: Workforce survey.

narrow conception of the union's role in society. They have vigorously pursued the political and social implications of technological change and the impact of new telecommunications technology. This, in turn, has helped to demonstrate the union's concern for the wider issue of youth unemployment. The union has also had a hand in establishing an Australian Technology Foundation, and one of its key officers is currently serving as a member of an official inquiry into the effects of technological change (Committee of Enquiry into Technological Change in Australia).[17] From the ATEA's standpoint the issue of new technology has fulfilled a number of functions: mobilisation of the membership, translating ideological concerns into practice, and raising the consciousness of the wider public.

A discontented membership and a politically left wing union do not necessarily result in what we have termed an independent action profile. Without sufficient power, a militant union posture would be likely to deflect dissatisfaction away from the management to the union leadership. It is, therefore, necessary to briefly discuss the relative power of the ATEA. According to Hyman and Fryer (1977: 155), union power has four major determinants: membership density, strategic power, workers' awareness of a divergence between their interests and those of management, and solidarity. Table 5.12 summarises our assessment of the power of the independent and dependent unions respectively.

In terms of union density, only the clerical unions have less than 90 per cent of eligible workers outside the union (ACOA 70 per cent, APSA 47

TABLE 5.12

Assessment of relative union power.

Union type	Objective Determinants		Subjective Determinants	
			Awareness of	
		Strategic	Divergent	
	Density	Power	Interests	Solidarity
Independent (ATEA)	High	High	High	High
Dependent (other unions)	High	High/Low	Low	Low

per cent). The UPCT operates the only closed shop, but the ATEA and APTU have close to 100 per cent membership density.

It is in the area of strategic power that the ATEA has a considerable advantage over the other unions. Disruption to the network is the best available indicator of strategic power.[18] Three of the unions – the APTU, ACOA, and APSA – have little involvement in the network, because members perform tasks ancillary to its operations. Strikes by either of these unions would have a negligible impact for a considerable period of time. Where industrial action is resorted to (and this is relatively rare), it takes the form of defensive bans, typically as a reaction to, or protest against. management initiatives.

Members of the ATPOA and UPCT operate various aspects of the network and therefore have a good deal of strategic power. However, this is diminished because of increasing automation and the reduced demand for telegram services. The ATEA, on the other hand, has the most strategic power because its members are responsible for maintaining the network.

The awareness of a divergence between the interests of management and workers has been dealt with previously (see pp.122–3). Briefly, conflict-consciousness was much higher amongst the ATEA membership. Solidarity is an amalgam of a number of factors: support for union officials, homogeneity of membership, and ease of mobilisation. Whereas most unions have a large proportion of their membership outside the organisation, the ATEA and ATPOA members are drawn mainly from within Telecom, thereby making for greater homogeneity. In interviews, consistently higher estimates of membership support for the union were forthcoming from ATEA job delegates and officials, with the possible exception of the UPCT.

The sub-branch type of shop floor organisation developed by the

ATEA appears to offer advantages for mobilisation not present where shop stewards have been established. This form of structure consists of up to eight people actively engaged in union affairs. The influence exerted by this formally constituted body exceeds that of one or two departmental shop stewards. ATEA officials estimated that upwards of 70 per cent of their sub-branches were effective in the role the union had devised for them. This compared with about 30 per cent indicated by officials of other unions in respect of the efficiency of their workplace representatives.

All unions, with the exception of the UCPT, have large portions of their membership outside the metropolitan area, and effective mobilisation presents problems. The ATEA is the only union to have overcome this problem to any extent: in country regions, sub-branches are connected to mass meetings in the metropolitan area through the telecommunications network. These members are able to listen to the speakers, contribute to the meeting, and vote on resolutions.

In summary, solidarity is greater among the ATEA members, and overall, it has far more power than the other unions. This advantage has, without doubt, been an influence on the willingness of officials and members to take industrial action. According to ATEA officers, success in these struggles was essential to maintain support and encourage further action. By contrast, the dependent unions are restrained by their comparatively weak strategic positions in the work process.

It is clear that dissatisfaction is not confined to ATEA members and that collective action by the dependent unions is a less realistic strategic option. Might we not expect, then, a higher level of individual expressions of discontent among these workers? Unfortunately this hypothesis cannot be fully explored owing to data inadequacies; however, labour turnover figures are available (Table 5.13) and accordingly merit examination.

Although there are problems in using labour turnover as an index of individual conflict, the data tends to support the hypothesis that members

TABLE 5.13

Labour turnover in Telecom Queensland, 1977–78

Skill group	1977 %	1978 %
Technical	3.2	3.1
Lines	4.5	3.7
Clerical	10.3	10.1
Operator	18.4	14.0

Source: Telecom Australia Annual Report, 1976–77 and 1977–78.

of the dependent unions (linesmen, clerks, and operators) express their discontent individually, rather than through the articulation of collective grievances against management. With the exception of the lines group, Table 5.13 shows that their turnover rate is considerably higher than that of the technicians. The relatively low turnover rate of the linesmen is largely attributable to the fact that these skills are not readily transferable to other business organisations. Job mobility is, therefore, considerably restricted. While it is possible for high levels of conflict to be expressed in both collective and individual ways (Fox, 1971: 82–83), the low turnover rate of the technicians suggests that, at least in this case, the collective and individual expressions of conflict are interchangeable.

Two characteristics of the overall pattern of industrial action remain to be explained: the predominance of bans and their concentration at the State level. The importance of membership involvement in the operation of the network was earlier linked to the strategic power of unions. For the dependent unions, who do not have this involvement, the ineffectiveness of strike action results in a reliance on bans. While the ATPOA and UPCT possess some strategic power, other factors contribute to greater use of this type of action. In the case of the former, low solidarity encourages industrial action that does not require a high level of participation by workers. The latter recognises the adverse effects of disruption on an already declining service. The ATEA, despite its strategic power, is deterred from the use of strikes by the capacity of the network to continue functioning for considerable periods without maintenance. Bans have the same effect but at little cost to the union or its members.[19]

The greater involvement of unions in industrial action over State as opposed to national issues is a result of the concentration of union power at the State branch level and difficulties of mobilisation across vast distances. In addition, by restricting action to the State, the more punitive legal sanctions brought into play by the National Government are likely to be avoided since, at least until now (January 1979), these have only applied to national disputes.

Conclusions

The emergence of low trust relations in Telecom has occurred as a result of management strategies which appear to be incompatible with the aspirations of the workforce. Predicated on an anachronistic ideology (mutual interests philosophy), management have attempted to satisfy new economic efficiency goals, only to find that this has evoked employee discontent, particularly among the technicians. The desire of these workers for high discretion work roles clashed with management's efforts to increase control as a means of improving economic efficiency. Members of the remaining occupational groups reported dissatisfaction, but the issues that concerned them were amenable to negotiation and arbitration through well established channels. Union officials responded in the conventional way, they have little option to do otherwise, given the amount of power at their disposal. Thus dependent unions were found to be characterised by a dependent action profile; one whose key feature is a low level of industrial action, typified by bans and protest stoppages.

The technicians' union, the ATEA, responded to the members' discontent in a non-conventional way. This, it was argued, was partly a consequence of the non-negotiable nature of the issues that were causing discontent among these workers. While it was possible for the union to redirect grievances over job control into channels more acceptable to management, the union did not choose to do so. Instead, the ATEA, consistent with its left wing ideology, adopted a militant posture. It was argued that this avenue was open to it because of the power at its disposal.Thus, this independent type of union was shown to be associated with what we termed the independent action profile. The key feature of this profile was a relatively high level of industrial action often in the form of aggressive bans.

Although the ATEA's organisation and style are different from the other unions in the telecommunications industry, this aoes not necessarily imply that a new form of unionism is emerging in Australia. Indeed, there is much similarity between the responses of these modern technicians and the craftsmen of yesteryear. Faced with undesirable technological and organisational changes, militant collectivism has been a common tendency, especially where this is buttressed by official union structures.

As for the future, much will depend on the willingness of management to change, or temper, its goals and adopt a new philosophy of industrial relations. This will require a good deal of thought, and discussion with the unions. Meanwhile, there are signs that the dependent unions are beginning to adopt a more militant posture and, furthermore, there is currently much speculation about union amalgamations. Clearly, these developments are likely to have far reaching consequences, perhaps they will provide the necessary impetus for the reform of industrial relations in the telecommunications industry.

NOTES

1.   Telecom constitutes the bulk of the telecommunications industry which is evident from the broad scope of its functions in conjunction with its monopoly position.
2.   In June 1978, Telecom employed 87 444 full-time staff, 13 609 (15.6 per cent) in Queensland.

3. The Public Service Board is the employing authority for all Federal Government departments.
4. According to Telecom Australia Annual Reports, labour productivity increased by approximately 9 per cent between 1976 and 1978. Employment has remained stable over the past four years.
5. Standardisation is defined as the degree to which specific procedures are followed in processing management decisions of various kinds. Formalisation denotes the existence of explicit written instructions or similar rules for these activities (Turner, C. Roberts and D. Roberts, 1977: 12).
6. Apart from the current trend towards computerised telephone exchanges, computers are also being introduced in the clerical area. A document entitled 'Implementation of the Corporate Plan, 1977' lists fourteen probable applications of computer technology affecting clerical work. The list is now much longer and will involve all four skill groups. In the lines area, technological change will drastically reduce the requirement for lines connecting subscribers to telephone exchanges, and the eventual use of fibre optics will revolutionise this aspect of lines work.
7. The power of the national officials has been eroded since the early seventies, following an unfavourable agreement concluded with management in 1969. Relations between State and Federal officials have become increasingly strained.
8. In part, this may be attributed to the more efficient data collection system in Queensland, but this factor is unlikely to account for most of the disparity in the figures.
9. This does not imply that industrial action is State-wide in scope. The majority of bans are confined to specific work areas.
10. The Human Relations school, characterised by the work of Australian-born Elton Mayo, covers a variety of management methods and devices aimed at creating socially harmonious relationships between management and workers. Much emphasis is placed on the development of a stable community at the workplace.
11. In summary, these factors include the relationships between the system of conciliation and arbitration, the Public Service Board, the enterprise and the unions, insulated as they were from private sector industrial relations. Extreme centralisation in these organisations, coupled with considerable integration of workers into the enterprise both ideologically and behaviourally, facilitated a high degree of stability. This was based on relatively high wages, favourable working conditions, and bureaucratic paternalism. These characteristics are typical of government departments.
12. In their study of British firms, Turner, Roberts and Roberts (1977) found standardisation and formalisation in management processes to be directly related to the level of strike incidence.
13. Commonwealth Employees (Redeployment and Retirement) Bill, 1979.
14. The survey comprised a questionnaire to 500 randomly selected workers from the four skill groups in Queensland. The overall response rate was 46.2 per cent.
15. This is not to say that in the conciliation process individual commissioners accept the distinction between industrial and managerial issues. The point is that, in terms of arbitral jurisdiction, they have no power to decide on managerial issues.
16. The issues involved in this dispute concerned the introduction of new technology and the consequent reorganisation of work. The seriousness of this dispute is indicated by the Prime Minister's involvement and the commencement of deregistration proceedings against the union. The effects of this bitter conflict continue to be felt by local management and workers.
17. The Myer's Inquiry into technological change was established by the National Government in 1978 to examine, report, and make recommendations on the process of technological change in Australian industry in order to maximise economic, social, and other benefits and minimise any possible adverse consequences.

18. The telephone network joins together all customers throughout Australia and also connects to the international system. The cables and transmission equipment associated with the network are also used for purposes such as telex and datel services and relaying television and radio programmes. The network is the central communications medium in Australia. It is extremely vulnerable to disruption through bans on maintenance of equipment.

19. Mallet speaks of a scientific approach to the organisation of industrial action by technical workers: 'Instead of launching open ended strikes which gravely endanger the purchasing power of the strikers, the union will use its thorough knowledge of the productive mechanisms of the firm to organise the systematic disruption of production' (1975: 71).

CHAPTER SIX

Patterns of Industrial Action: Analysis and Conclusions*

Stephen J. Frenkel

This final chapter is concerned with the comparative analysis of industrial action based on the foregoing case studies. These studies demand answers to such questions as: to what extent are the industrial action patterns in the four industries alike; are there a number of common structural factors that help to explain both the similarities and differences between the industrial action profiles? In other words, is it possible to formulate a theory of industrial action, or are we simply left with a series of *ad hoc* explanations? It will be argued that our research does indeed point towards a theory. After exploring this aspect in some detail, consideration will be given to the research and policy implications of the theory. But first a number of potential criticisms of the case studies must be examined, for these may seriously detract from the force of our subsequent argument.

The Research: Some Critical Issues

There are six general problems, which are perhaps better expressed in the form of questions. Firstly, does the small number of industries limit the general applicability of the conclusions that can be drawn? In a similar vein, are the common denominators of industrial action, and hence the type of explanation offered, specific to a period of recession coupled with relatively high inflation? Thirdly, does it matter a great deal that the case studies are based on industries in different localities? Fourthly, how much reliance can be placed on the industry studies, given the limited resources that were available to the researchers? Fifthly, to what extent has the analytical framework and research methods biased our enquiries so that

*The contributors to this volume provided helpful comments on earlier drafts of this chapter but they should not be held responsible for any errors or blemishes; these are mine alone.

one or more potentially important explanatory variables have been neglected? And finally, how much reliance can be placed on the use of our industrial action data for purposes of comparison? These are, after all, drawn from various sources and are likely to understate the incidence of certain forms of industrial action. Each issue will be tackled in turn.

Just as one swallow does not make a summer, so the generality of our conclusions, based as they are on a small number of case studies, must be treated with caution. However, in as much as our theory is not contradicted by other relevant research findings (and we do not think this is the case), then it seems reasonable to claim some improvement on previous explanations. This implies that we do not believe the prevailing political-economic conditions unduly limit the content of our theory. This is partly because the theory is pitched at a relatively high level of abstraction: a more precise specification of the variables and their interrelationships would require the formulation of more detailed types of political-economic environments, including their empirical investigation. Although this may prove fruitful, it does not necessarily invalidate a more general theory that serves as a starting point for further detailed studies.

The problem of variations in community contexts is probably less of substantive than methodological significance. Though it would have been ideal to standardise the locale in which the research was undertaken, this was simply not possible. The industry studies are effectively based on industrial action concentrated in large urban centres: we have no reason to believe the data and accompanying analyses would be much different had we 'controlled for' the community context. But, like the possible impact of the specific political-economic environment, this can only be tested through further research.

The limited resources argument and that concerning possible bias imposed by the theoretical framework can be evaluated together. It would be ridiculous to deny that a great deal more could be said about industrial action in the four industries had sufficient resources been available to enable more empirical research to be undertaken. But we are reasonably convinced that the pictures painted in the previous chapters are valid, albeit limited representations of reality. The industries were in fact the subject of a seminar attended by eighty managers, union officials, tribunal members, civil servants, and academics prior to publication. There was a general consensus on our research findings, though where particular points of difference or error emerged, these were subsequently investigated and, where necessary, corrected and incorporated into this volume. In sum, we do not think that resource constraints or theoretical predilections seriously jeopardised the project.

It would be wrong to suppose that the studies do not contain certain 'blind spots'. With the possible exception of the telecommunications industry, the roles of employers' associations and senior management are insufficently understood. Despite attempts to elicit information concerning employers' strategy and tactics, including the relationships between business organisations and governments, such data was, perhaps not surprisingly, difficult to obtain. From the information at our disposal it appears that employers' associations and corporations typically play a significant role in supporting the general accommodation system and very probably are associated with many of the changes in the legislation; it is not possible to say much more than this. Our studies do, however, support the contention that Australian management rarely pursues *overt* industrial relations strategies except in response to union or, less frequently, government initiatives. They prefer to simply follow the codes of behaviour and norms required by the law and custom and practice. If, therefore, the role of employers fails to find a more important place in our theory, it is partly because of data inadequacies and partly on account of management dependence on the state in the field of industrial relations.

The inter-industry analysis being attempted here depends on drawing conclusions from reliable and essentially comparable data. On both criteria there are problems with forms of industrial action other than stoppages. These tend to be excluded in the waterfront data (p.92), while the Weekly Reports from which most of the construction, and shipbuilding and shiprepair (hereafter shipbuilding) data are derived, very probably understate the incidence of bans and other partial withdrawals of labour just as they do short, small strikes. We have, therefore, decided to exclude industrial tactics other than strikes from the subsequent analysis, except in relation to the telecommunications industry (hereafter Telecom) where bans are undoubtedly very significant.

The comparability criterion requires that data be collected for similar periods, but in this respect there is some variation in our case studies. The analysis of construction mainly covers the years 1976–78, shipbuilding and Telecom 1975–78, and the waterfront study spans the decade 1969–78. Although standardisation of the base period was thought to be important, this had to be balanced against considerations specific to each industry. In the case of construction, the year 1975 was excluded since it was a climactic period, and the small size of the waterfront industry required a sufficient number of disputes to permit generalisation. A four-year time span was insufficient for this purpose.

These two variations do not detract from the subsequent analysis: a random check on the 1975 construction data gives no grounds for altering the conclusions reached in Chapter Two. Similarly, there is considerable consistency in the waterfront dispute pattern over the decade 1969–78 (pp.89–94). Nevertheless, variations in both the base period and the sources of information caution against making distinctions that place too great a burden on the data.

Accordingly, emphasis will be given to those dimensions of industrial action that unambiguously illustrate the similarities and differences in the dispute patterns.

Inter-Industry Comparisons of Industrial Action Profiles

In order to facilitate analysis, Table 6.1 presents in summary form the main empirical features of the industrial action patterns found in the four industries, together with the exceptions to these common characteristics.

TABLE 6.1

Industrial action in four industries: similarities and exceptions

Industrial action dimensions	Common features	Exceptions
Incidence	Relatively high	Construction
Types of work stoppage	Mainly autonomous	Telecom
	Some campaign strikes	–
	Stop-work meetings	–
Location	Large establishments in metropolitan centres	Telecom
Issues	Pay	Telecom
	Management policy and behaviour	Waterfront
	Demarcation	Telecom
	Intra-union communication	–
Duration	Short strikes (2 days or less)	–
	Long bans (more than 5 days)	–
Intra-industry variations in union militancy	Large	Waterfront

Source: Industry case studies.

Notwithstanding certain aspects of the Telecom dispute profile, there is a comparatively high degree of correspondence between the patterns of industrial action in the four industries. Leaving aside the exceptions for a moment, the prevailing features include a relatively high incidence of autonomous type disputes and a much smaller proportion of larger campaign stoppages and stop-work meetings. Labour conflicts tend to concentrate in large establishments located in metropolitan centres. These focus on three main types of issues: pay; management policy and behaviour concerning labour utilisation and control; and demarcation. Communicating with members at meetings also accounts for some 'lost' time.

Strikes are generally of short duration (two days or less), and bans tend to be a good deal longer (over five days). The case studies also indicate that there are considerable variations in militancy between members of different unions in the same industry.

A useful theory of industrial action is one that is capable of explaining the exceptions as well as the common denominators of the dispute patterns. These can be briefly recounted by reference to Table 6.1

Construction in the period under review was shown to be no more dispute-prone than might be expected from its relative share of employment (p.32). Industrial action in Telecom, on the other hand, displayed a number of features at variance with the common pattern. These included numerous bans imposed by technicians working in small mobile groups focusing almost solely on control issues. Conflicts over pay and demarcation were found to be very infrequent.

The waterfront dispute profile differed from the general pattern in two main respects: very few conflicts occurred over management policy and behaviour, and greater occupational homogeneity precludes a comparative analysis of inter-union militancy.

A Theory of Industrial Action

The existence of common dispute features suggests the presence of similar structural factors and social responses in the industries under examination. By the same token, the exceptions noted above should be explicable in terms of variations in structural properties or social action or both. Figure 6.1 provides a basis for exploring these propositions.

The theory summarised in Figure 6.1 focuses attention on the dialectical relationship between three sets of factors: workers' discontent and power, union structure and character, and the accommodation structure pertaining to that industry. The first of these elements is largely conditioned by the prevailing mode of production. To a lesser extent these aspects are influenced by current union structure, which might facilitate or retard resolution of workplace problems, and the role of the state. Accordingly, governments and statutory organisations may act provocatively or in a manner conducive to resolving workers' problems.

FIGURE 6.1

Schematic representation of industrial action theory

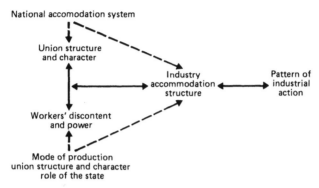

Although one among three key structural influences on workers' discontent and power, union structure and character has a significant direct impact on patterns of industrial action. By structure and character we mean the inter-organisational and intra-organisational features of labour organisations. These include their membership coverage, size, method of government, policies, and relations between leaders and members. The principal influence on these aspects are the procedural rules — both past and present — that regulate the national industrial relations system.

The accommodation structures of the particular industries under consideration constitute the third building block in our theory. The relevant awards, agreements, and statutes effectively define the rules of the game. They set the parameters that are considered to be publicly legitimate. The accommodation structure also provides the inducements and sanctions that enter into the strategic calculations and hence influence the actions of the participants. These institutional arrangements are the product of many historical and current factors, the most significant of which include the national accommodation system, the mode of production, union structure, and the role of the state.

The subsequent analysis will try to show that the sources of workers' discontent and power in the four industries stem from similar underlying structural problems and that there are strong parallels with regard to union structures and strategies. Furthermore, accommodation structures tend to resemble one another. The interaction of these similar structural factors helps to explain the common elements in the dispute patterns, while discrepancies in certain aspects of the three aforementioned factors account for the exceptions to the patterns noted earlier in Table 6.1.

Worker Discontent and Power

It may be helpful to begin by recalling the major sources of worker discontent in the four industries. The evidence from construction pointed towards instability of employment and pressure exerted by management in the pursuit of greater profitability. In shipbuilding, job insecurity and earnings fluctuations appeared to be significant sources of disquiet, while uncertainty regarding the nature of future employment and low trust of management characterised workers' sense of deprivation on the water-front and in Telecom. Dissatisfaction assumes a potentially more radical form on the waterfront where 15.2 per cent of working days 'lost' through disputes concern wider social or political issues (Table 4.4, p.93). In telecommunications, conflict over job control, especially amongst the technicians, has been magnified to include widespread disaffection with Telecom's decision-making system and the assumptions on which it is based.

As far as workers' sense of injustice is concerned, two basic threads seem to run through the four industries: employment insecurity and inadequate job control. These are key aspects of alienation that stem from structural properties of the capitalist mode of production, though, it should be added, by no means confined to that system (see Haraszti, 1977). Nonetheless, the pursuit of profit under market conditions and private property relations entails the use of labour as a resource to be employed at the discretion of, and in the manner desired by, management, subject only to the formal and informal rules included in statutes, awards, and agreements.

Widespread discontent may be a necessary, but not sufficient, condition for translation into industrial action. For this to occur on a recurrent basis, strategic, motivational, and organisational resources are required in order that sanctions can be effectively wielded against management. This issue may be usefully tackled in a comparative way by employing the four-dimensional concept of power initially developed by Hyman and Fryer (1977) and also utilised by Muller (pp.125–6). Table 6.2 presents a crude summary of the relevant information.

High union density is a feature of the four industries; no sector has less than 70 per cent of the manual labour force in one or more unions. In terms of strategic position, construction, shipbuilding, and the waterfront are associated with large capital units that can easily be rendered unpro-ductive. High fixed costs and costly contract provisions ensure that delays in production are minimised so that buildings and ships can begin earning revenue. Competitive product markets are a further incentive for manage-ment to take labour demands seriously: loss of only a few future orders may seriously jeopardise a firm's existence. In telecommunications, it is

TABLE 6.2

Comparative union power at workplace level
in four industries

	Industry			
Power	Construction	Shipbuilding	Waterfront	Telecom
Objective facets				
Density	High	High	High	High
Strategic position	High	High	High	High/Low
Subjective facets				
Conflict consciousness	High	High	High	High*
Solidarity	High*	High*	High	High/Low

*Indicates some disparity in comparison with the other industries similarly designated.

the capacity to interrupt a vital and virtually non-substitutable community service that confers strategic power on certain groups of workers. Other groups are less well placed, hence the designation 'high/low' in Table 6.2.

On the first subjective dimension of power, conflict consciousness, data based on industrial disputes and questionnaires in the construction and shipbuilding industries indicated that workers were well aware of their precarious economic situation and hence their perceived need for protection against the vagaries of the market and management power. On the waterfront, a highly developed conflict consciousness is illustrated by the suspicion with which workers regard the companies (p.95 and Turkington 1976: 271–274) and the extent to which they are prepared to engage in struggles over wider social and political issues. Telecommunications workers also show little trust in management, and a large number believe that industrial action is often necessary to obtain consideration of their interests (Table 5.8 p.122). These and other data point towards a relatively highly developed awareness of conflicting interests, especially amongst technicians. However, this aspect has been designated with an asterisk in Table 6.2, acknowledging that telecommunication workers are probably a good deal less conflict conscious than their counterparts in the three traditional working class industries.

In the case of shipbuilding, the traditional correspondence between occupational groups and unions, coupled with the declining volume of work, has reinforced a particularistic solidarity; hence the asterisk in Table 6.2, indicating a very high degree of intra-occupational solidarity. Construction workers, on the other hand, have been experiencing a reduction in solidarity with the long term decline in skill levels, the growth of

sub-contracting, and the relative weakness of unionism in the home building sub-sector. Accordingly, the asterisk in Table 6.2 denotes this
qualification placed on their high solidarity.

The waterfront is characterised by a strong sense of cohesion, but, by
contrast, Telecom workers appear to place much less emphasis on collectivism, consistent with the bureaucratic predilections and strategies of
management. The technicians are somewhat atypical, and the ATEA is
striving to support tendencies towards militant collectivism by laying the
foundations for stronger workplace organisation.

On the basis of this brief analysis, it is reasonable to argue that, at
workplace level, workers in three of our four industries possess sufficient
resources to mount collective struggles against management. In the case
of Telecom, the workers' position is more ambiguous on account of
variations between occupational groups; a topic we shall be discussing in
more detail later. Nevertheless, as a preliminary conclusion, it is clear that
the two conditions facilitating recurrent industrial action are present in
the four industries: worker discontent of the kind that cannot easily be
resolved on an individual basis and a degree of power sufficient to engage
in industrial struggle.

Union Structure and Character

It is typically through recourse to trade union norms, symbols, and
officials (both lay and full-time) that industrial action is organised and
legitimated. Indeed, we wish to argue that the similarities in union structure and character in the four industries exert a powerful influence on the
organisational attributes of industrial action. But first these common
elements must be demonstrated and explained. This is best accomplished
by distinguishing between four major features of union structure and
behaviour density; the number and types of unions in the industry; the
ideological orientation of the unions; and inter-union and intra-union
relations.

In the discussion of workers' power, we noted that high density of
unions was common to the four industries. With regard to the number of
unions, the case studies indicated that there were a large number of unions
in each industry: there are eleven unions in construction and over twenty
in the three remaining industries. This fragmentation is associated with
the occupational basis of most Australian unions, while one of the consequences of the 1951 New Zealand waterfront dispute was the splitting of
the Waterside Workers' Union into a host of port unions (p.86).
Similar ideological divisions characterise the unions in the four industries:
communist, democratic socialist, and social democratic forces are represented. With the exception of Telecom, the predominant unions
(measured in terms of membership size) tend to be on the left of the

political spectrum. This means that many union leaders are predisposed towards militant strategies. It is also worth noting that the AMWSU, BWIU, and NZWWF continue to provide some of the leading lights in the left wing political parties.

Again with the exception of Telecom, demarcation disputes have been commonplace in the industries under review. Political differences often underly these struggles for job territory, while personal and organisational loyalties contribute to the especial bitterness of these conflicts.

Intra-union relations have a tendency towards instability. Thus, during the course of our analysis of the construction industry, we noted the factional strife associated with the BLF, the AWU, the Plumbers, and the Electricians (pp.50-60), while reference was made in the Telecom study to strained relations between the ATEA State and Federal bodies (p.130 f.n.7). Internal union conflict in the waterfront industry is moderated by the substantial autonomy vested in the port unions, but in shipbuilding relations between workplace unions and State level organisations is made difficult by the strength of work-units and shop steward substructures, coupled with the fact that the unions organising these workers have, in the main, a very small proportion of their total membership employed in the shipbuilding industry. Consequently, full-time officers tend to pay less attention to this sector.

The principal explanations for the inter-industry similarities in union structure and character lie in the interrelationships between the historical traditions of the Australian labour movement and the general accommodation structure, which regulated (and continues to constrain) union behaviour. Both were conditioned by the geographical context in which unions developed and persisted.

Many Australian unions trace their origins back to the craft organisations established by British immigrants in the nineteenth century. These organisations probably established a tradition of job consciousness, since unilateral regulation was the preferred method of protecting tradesmen's employment and earnings (see Clegg, 1979: 19-20). The emergence of conciliation and arbitration arrangements in the late nineteenth and early twentieth centuries perpetuated the occupational basis of trade unionism, leading to a great many different unions as new semi-skilled, skilled, and white collar occupations emerged. The geographical dispersion of the working population also contributed to the large number of relatively independent centres of union power, while union density was fostered by State and Federal Tribunals. These simply could not work without employees being represented at hearings by labour organisations. Moreover, certain trades enjoyed a favourable market position, so their bargaining power was sufficient to ensure a *de facto* closed shop in large urban areas.

The presence of militant and moderate unions in the same industry is characteristic of Australia generally. Two main factors account for this: the first is the dominant roles that governments, tribunals, and courts have played in industrial relations; the second is the way in which management and unions regulate their relations. Because the ground rules of the accommodation system are strongly influenced by governments, it follows that unions will take a keen interest in politics by attempting to ensure that a government favourable to their interests is elected or returned to office. Australian unions are especially political since, under a Federal constitutional system, they are capable of influencing both State and Federal administrations.

The various systems of accommodation confer membership coverage rights on particular unions; however, it is not uncommon for several unions to have jurisdiction over the same occupational categories. We cannot enter into a discussion of the reasons for this here, but suffice it to note that management have not infrequently taken advantage of this type of situation to encourage employees to join moderate unions. This has accentuated inter-union bitterness, especially where small or weak right wing unions are dependent on their more militant counterparts and the tribunals for securing improvements in award wages and conditions. Accusations of 'being in the bosses' pocket' are counteracted with criticisms of 'mindless militancy'.

There is a tendency towards concentration of decision-making power at a regional, (State branch) rather than workplace or national, level in most Australian unions. This is related to the emergence of densely populated urban areas around the six capital cities, which are separated by long distances. The small size of plants has constrained the development of strong workplace organisations, though shop stewards are important in certain industries where establishment size, market uncertainty, and strong union traditions provide favourable ingredients for their consolidation. On the other hand, there has been a continuing thrust towards greater centralisation of union decision-making. Governments, tribunals, and employers associations tend to favour standardising the wage determination process at national level. The main consequence of these varying influences on unions has been to confuse and further diversify union decision-making power: one of the prime reasons for the weak control systems characteristic of Australian unions.

Factionalism is facilitated by this feature of union decision-making structures, while the political character of the labour movement provides a basis for the alignment of opposing forces. Of particular significance are the requirements of the conciliation and arbitration statutes, which provide for regular elections for full-time positions (Sorrell, 1979: 159–170).

In sum, the broad characteristics of the unions in our four industries are similar and differ only in degree from those of others in the Australian labour movement. As we have argued, these can be traced back to historical, geographical, and institutional factors.

Accommodation Structures: Common Features

With the exception of the waterfront, the three remaining industries are substantially regulated by the Federal conciliation and arbitration legislation and its institutional machinery. This makes for uniformity in the industrial relations practices of these industries. The common denominators of the accommodation structures in these industries, together with that of the waterfront, can be elucidated by focusing on four facets of these arrangements. These are: the dominant mode of regulation, including the perceived legitimacy of the procedural rules *vis à vis* industrial action; the approximate number of representative organisations involved in the primary awards or agreements; the number of such awards and agreements; and the extent of centralisation and formalisation of these instruments, including their issue-scope, that is, the extent to which they provide for joint regulation.

Compulsory conciliation and arbitration is the common form of regulation in all four industries, though the institutions administering the New Zealand waterfront are arguably more representative than their Australian counterparts. Compulsion neither facilitates consensus rule-making nor responsibility for rule enforcement. Thus, with some exceptions, trade union leaders show little commitment to the prevention of industrial action, even though this type of activity is often illegal. The exceptions include agreements and awards that are substantially the product of collective bargaining under no undue duress; the most recent construction industry tradesmen's award (1979) would probably fall into this category. The legitimacy of accommodation structures is also enhanced in the eyes of union leaders by state intervention to regulate the power of employers. The WIC in the waterfront industry is a tripartite statutory body which, according to Turkington, has effectively assumed many of the industrial relations functions of management (p.95).

By and large, however, restraint by conflict conscious workers and militant unions' leaders has been secured via the efficacy of the substantive rules. High wages and improved conditions have tended to prevent massive confrontations, but, paradoxically, the belief has been perpetuated that favourable arbitration decisions are only forthcoming when backed by industrial muscle.

The relevant number of major representative organisations and primary regulative instruments is set out in Table 6.3 on the following page. Several important points emerge from a cursory inspection of this table. Firstly, there are considerably fewer major employers associations

TABLE 6.3

Representative organisations and primary regulative instruments in four industries

	Construction	Shipbuilding	Waterfront	Telecom
Number of major :				
employer				
organisations*	4	3	2	2
trade unions	7	8	19	5
statutory bodies**	2	3	4	1
Number of primary :				
statutes, awards,				
agreements	7	6+	3+	8

*Excludes individual employers unless these are very large.
**Excludes legal institutions which rarely deal with industrial relations problems.

Source: Industry case studies.

than unions in each industry, indicating the higher degree of fragmentation on the labour side, although caution should be exercised in comparing these two dissimilar types of organisations. Secondly, there is a parallel between the industries in the relatively high formal involvement of statutory bodies in industrial relations, bearing in mind that not all the various courts are included in the figures. Thirdly, a large number of regulative instruments characterise industrial relations in the four industries, reflecting in large measure the fragmentation of the trade unions. The importance of formal port agreements and yard understandings on the waterfront and in shipbuilding respectively is indicated by the plus signs in Table 6.3; their exact number is impossible to estimate.

What Table 6.3 fails to show is the union level at which the formal procedural and substantive rules are forged. With the exception of the waterfront, these tend to be made above the workplace, although stewards will typically accompany full-time union officials in award hearings and negotiations. Given the large amount of statutory machinery, it comes as no surprise to find that the major regulative instruments in all four industries generally take the form of statutes and awards rather than collective agreements. These are typically highly detailed and expressed in language virtually impossible for the average worker to understand. Finally, with regard to the extent of joint regulation or issue-scope, awards tend to be narrow. This is related to the constitutional inability of tribunals in all but the waterfront industry to arbitrate on managerial prerogative issues such as hiring, transfers, and dismissal of workers. In practice, however, agreements are made, although employers are especially sensitive to sharing power.

Even allowing for the exceptions, it is quite clear that there is a significant degree of correspondence among the accommodation structures in the four industries. What remains to be explained is how these, and the other similarities noted in respect of workers' discontent and power, and union characteristics, interrelate to create the common features of the industrial action patterns described earlier (pp.135–6). In the same way the exceptions to the general pattern also require explanation.

Explaining the Similarities and Differences in the Industrial Action Patterns

Using Table 6.1 as the explanatory reference point, we might commence our analysis by asking why three of the four industries tend to experience a comparatively high incidence of disputes. An appropriate response would be that workers in these industries are particularly sensitive to the high level of actual or anticipated work instability, and they possess the power to express their discontent and support their claims with collective action. This capacity to mobilise resources is used largely in defence; it is significantly under-utilised in respect of programmes for workplace reform and rule administration.

Union leaders exercise little restraint on the rank and file for they, by and large, either support this 'sparkplug' militancy (Shorter and Tilly, 1974: 180–184) in order to cultivate a more vigorous workplace unionism, or they accommodate pragmatically to such activity with little expectation that things might be different. Union officials tend to disregard the procedural rules for several reasons: firstly, because it is expedient to do so, bearing in mind that union elections are never far away; secondly, because these officers are not responsible for their authorship; and thirdly, they can escape the consequences of their actions by focusing criticism on these statutory bodies. And as noted earlier, many union officials believe that employers and tribunals will not accede to new union demands unless pressured to do so.

The construction industry did not prove to be highly dispute-prone, despite considerable work instability. It was argued that there were offsetting features associated with the mode of production (high unemployment and the changing composition of demand), trade union behaviour (political reciprocity with a Labor Government), and the accommodation structure (favourable substantive rules and centralisation). These factors were conducive to the current low level of industrial action in this industry.

It is well known that the vast majority of disputes in Australia do not involve very large numbers of workers (Frenkel, 1978b); this is no less true of the four industries under examination. The principal explanation for the predominance of what Frenkel and Coolican have termed 'autonomous type conflicts' is to be found in the nature of union structure and the dynamics of the accommodation systems.

In order to illustrate the cogency of this argument it is useful to approach this question by asking why broader struggles, that is, campaign type disputes, are so rare. There are three main aspects of union structure that militate against these more comprehensive forms of conflict. Firstly, occupationally fragmented unions, many of which are small and inefficient, simply do not possess the human and financial resources to organise large scale campaigns. Secondly, the dispersion of union members over a wide variety of industries, together with the decline of craft consciousness in the modern era, makes large scale worker mobilisation for any length of time extremely difficult. Thirdly, State-wide industry campaigns are hampered by the large number of unions in each of the four industries; moreover, co-ordination problems are exacerbated by inter-union competition and mistrust, as well as intra-union factionalism. Nation-wide struggles on an industry or occupational basis are even more problematic given the tendency towards concentration of union decision-making power at State branch rather than national level.

Since wide-area struggles are difficult to promote, unions have resorted to autonomous and domestic type conflicts. As previously noted, these are confined to a single workplace and represent expressions of discontent and claims for improvement by work groups who are generally members of the same union. The waterfront is a variation of a theme rather than an exception, a point we shall return to shortly. The generally narrow organisational scope of industrial action can be further comprehended by noting the impact of accommodation structures on industrial relations behaviour.

The compulsory conciliation and arbitration system not only discourages rank and file control by union officials, it also promotes *anomie* (normlessness) at workplace level (Fox and Flanders, 1969: 247). With the emphasis placed on regulation above the workplace, and the highly formalised nature of awards and statutes, shop steward organisations tend to be ephemeral and weak. However, where structural factors such as size of establishment and strategic position confer power on work groups, shop committees have developed and persisted. Thus in construction, shipbuilding, and several other industries (see Frenkel 1978a; 1980); management has been forced to negotiate with workers' immediate representatives. But the authority of shop stewards and their committees is only grudgingly accepted by commissioners, judges, and many union officials, as is evident from the meagre facilities afforded to them. This means that formal joint regulation at workplace level remains rudimentary and un-even. Without authoritative shop steward organisations, militant work groups are able to pursue their sectional interests by taking industrial action with relative impunity.

Although autonomous disputes constitute the largest category in both the construction and shipbuilding industries, domestic struggles are also relatively common (pp.35 and 72). The multi-union character of these conflicts is facilitated by three aspects of work and union organisation. These include administrative and work processes that encourage members of different unions to associate with one another, the emergence of shop steward organisation aimed at unifying workers at the same workplace, and attempts by union officials to promote inter-union solidarity.

The waterfront is a variation on the autonomous conflict theme in that, while most disputes involve only one union, these are practically all establishment-wide in scope; in contrast to the sectional character of most industrial action in the other three industries. This difference is explained largely by the structure and character of trade unionism on the waterfront.

The existence of eighteen independent unions militates against struggles encompassing a large number of ports, or nation-wide action, but it does imply that full-time officers are close at hand to resolve workplace problems. The authority of these officials is bolstered by the large number of agreements they conclude at this level (p.97), as well as their expert knowledge of the complex industry-wide award. It would appear that sectional industrial action is discouraged in favour of port-wide mass meetings, where decisions on key issues are made (p.96). In this context it is noteworthy that the job delegate role is a relatively minor one, partly for reasons associated with the nature of work organisation (p.96), but also because the unions have seen little need to expand it. Furthermore, in contrast to shipbuilding, it has not developed in response to formal accommodation systems and official union structures imperfectly suited to the mode of production.

So far our analysis has concentrated on strike frequency; however, it should be borne in mind that, although single and multi-union campaign stoppages are few in number, they account for a substantial proportion of working days 'lost' in the four industries. As Frenkel and Coolican argue in Chapter Two, these types of disputes are closely related to the contours of industry awards and agreements, while also reflecting the ideologies and strategies of the unions.

Although we do not wish to dwell on form as an aspect of industrial patterns, for reasons referred to earlier (p.134), some comment on strikes is necessary, since this form of industrial action, data problems notwith-standing, appears to be the most popular in three of our four industries. Why should this be so?

In the first place strikes in these industries are likely to be effective: a lightning, or unpredicted, stoppage can be extremely costly, so management are often forced to negotiate and are willing to resolve a problem in the least possible time. Other forms of action, including bans, stop-work meetings, and various types of output restriction, are generally less dramatic in their consequences and are frequently employed as preliminary tactics to 'soften management up'. Even where alternative forms of action are more effective, strikes are common because tactics such as rolling stoppages, or what the Italians term 'chequerboard strikes' (Low-Beer, 1978: 48), are more difficult to organise. These generally require reasonably efficient workplace substructures or the presence of full-time officials.

From the standpoint of the union officials, strikes also have certain advantages over other forms of struggle. They are easier to respond to, being a familiar and more legitimate form of action. Small scale strikes are also much more simple to organise and control; other forms of action may lead to sectional conflicts among workers, or be exploited by management to change the basis of disputes. Last but not least, union officials frequently make the point that if management wishes to escalate a conflict from a partial withdrawl of labour to a strike, they can usually do so quite easily: by instantly dismissing one or more 'ringleaders' unions are typically forced to respond by calling for strike action.

This discussion leads to a consideration of the nature and common use of bans rather than strikes in Telecom. Workers in this industry have not yet sufficiently distanced themselves psychologically from management, so that industrial action has not attained the same legitimacy in the eyes of the Telecom workers as in the older working class sectors. Moreover, the bureaucratic nature of Telecom, with its emphasis on life-time careers, suggests that recalcitrant individuals may be subject to subtle discrimination. For these reasons, much greater reliance is placed on full-time union officials in the conduct of industrial action than in construction or shipbuilding. But it would be a mistake to assume that most disputes are engineered by the leadership; rather, like the waterfront, full-time officials are engaged in managing manifest discontent. But unlike the waterfront, this is triggered periodically by management behaviour. The division of labour and the presence of distinct occupational unions ensures that the great majority of bans fall into the autonomous dispute category.

Bans are more common than strikes in Telecom because industrial action in this industry is still regarded with ambivalence by workers and strongly repudiated by management. It is not simply a fact of life to which managers, as in other industries, have grown accustomed. Neither is the strategic position of even the most favourably placed workers so superior that strike action is likely to immediately bring management to the bargaining table (p.126). Indeed, given the precarious balance of power which, with government intervention, might easily go against the unions, both union officials and workers are wary of escalation that could be so massive as to jeopardise the existence of their organisations.

These conditions that limit workers' power have influenced the strategy and tactics of the unions in this industry. Bans are preferred by union officials, since they are able to supervise their application. Indeed, ATEA officers are particularly well placed to assume a regular leadership role, since this union organises solely within the telecommunications industry. Bans usually involve key groups of loyal union members, so reliance on a possibly hesitant membership is minimised, and management is not provoked into taking large scale retaliatory measures.

Our discussion of types of work stoppages would be incomplete without some comment on the large number of unauthorised union meetings in all but the telecommunications industry. These exemplify expediency, union inefficiency, and lack of management co-operation.

It is well known that union branch meetings are poorly attended. Although these remain the most important formal channel through which members exercise some influence on union decision-making, this function has been increasingly replaced by workplace meetings, which are called as the need arises. These are usually held in lunch or tea break periods, more often than not with the relevant full-time union officials in attendance. Awards do provide for authorised meetings, typically specifying the maximum period per week that may be used for this purpose, however, the unions generally pay little attention to this rule. Telecom is more generous with the time allowed for workplace union meetings,[1] this being the main reason for the smaller number of unauthorised stoppages of this kind. By contrast, in shipbuilding and the waterfront, stop-work meetings are so much a part of custom and practice that certain unions, like the Painters and Dockers and the various port unions on the waterfront, use such occasions to conduct Branch business.

Meetings can be run efficiently, avoiding lost time and deductions from wages. However, our first hand observations suggest that in this respect union meetings leave much to be desired. In part, this is due to inadequate planning, but more particularly because mass meetings are used to debate strategy or tactics, functions for which they are clearly unsuited. Furthermore, lack of resources, such as adequate meeting places, and amplification systems, create further serious problems.

Management have generally done little to assist in making union meetings more effective, partly because the various awards do not require such co-operation, but also on account of the belief that the provision of better facilities would serve to prolong these meetings, strengthen the hand of union militants, or both. Whatever the merits or otherwise of these arguments, these inadequacies illustrate the low priority given to decentralised accommodation arrangements.

Turning now to the location of industrial action, it is evident that large workplaces situated in metropolitan centres are most susceptible to disputes. The Telecom technicians are, to some extent, an exception, for which there is a simple explanation: although these workers work in small groups, they enjoy considerable autonomy *and* have access to a communications system that puts them in instant contact with both colleagues and union officials. The telephone and telex network, therefore, acts as a substitute for the face to face contact that is found in more conventional workplaces.

In another respect, the technicians are not dissimilar to their counterparts who work in large establishments: both sets of workers experience impersonal standardised rules created and changed by inaccessible officials according to criteria that appear to have less to do with human welfare than economic efficiency.

There are several further aspects of large workplaces that facilitate trade unionism and industrial action. Large workplaces tend to be organisationally and culturally more complex, thereby generating a greater number of labour problems. It is, therefore, convenient for management to negotiate with workers' representatives in order to resolve problems expeditiously. Shop steward substructures tend to develop as bargaining becomes institutionalised. Workplace bargaining also encourages work groups to use their strategic power, which, if employed to obtain sectional improvements, can upset relativities and stimulate further industrial action (Fox and Flanders, 1969: 151–180). The considerable amount of capital tied up in large operations, or the nature of technology, or both, frequently facilitates the use of industrial action, either by work groups or as part of (restricted) campaign type conflicts orchestrated by union leaders. Indeed, union officials generally pay more attention to the larger workplaces, where they have developed strong relationships with trusted stewards as a result of regular visits to the workplace. The greater receptivity to trade unionism among workers in large workplaces reinforces the influence of a counter ideology or subordinate meaning system (Parkin, 1971; Batstone *et al.*, 1977: 122–130) fostered by union officials and experienced job delegates. This places the use of industrial action in a more or less coherent ideological framework. In this way industrial struggle acquires legitimacy in the eyes of the workers. But these processes are by no means inevitable, for, as the Telecom study shows, there are ways in which large commercial organisations may be structured in order to minimise the role of trade unionism. Indeed, this may well be one of the main goals of current experiments in worker participation and organisational redesign.

So far, nothing has been said about the impact of community factors on the incidence of industrial action. It is indeed difficult to assess their influence, since no systematic comparisons were made between the principal metropolitan contexts and less complex and more sparsely populated areas. Nor would this be an easy task, since the reporting of industrial action in less densely populated areas is much more haphazard than in the major cities, where officials of the Department of Industrial Relations keep a keen eye on the industrial scene. Notwithstanding these observations, it is common for union officials to argue that unionism is a dirty word in 'the country' and that organising outside the large urban centres is exceptionally difficult. Although non-unionised workers have been known to engage in industrial action (Stearns, 1971: 122), our union sources indicate that such activity is very rare, even in major cities. As a tentative conclusion, we suggest that workplace factors or rather factors associated with the mode of production are more significant, since it is these that provide the main influence on the community context. In other words workers in small towns, and even some cities outside the metropolitan centres, are likely to articulate anti-union attitudes because industry is on such a small scale and often within a larger agricultural context. Class awareness is suppressed by the dominant ideology, which fosters status consciousness. This is reinforced by visible income and prestige differences (Wild, 1974: 119–129). Under conditions such as these, unions find it difficult to secure a footing and supply an alternative interpretation of everyday work life, which in turn would provide a vocabulary of motive (Mills, 1963: 439–452) for engaging in industrial action.

While the mode of production appears to be the principal factor explaining the location of industrial action, its significance in relation to the issues precipitating industrial action is less obvious. Here the roles of accommodation and union structures must be acknowledged. With the exception of Telecom, between approximately a quarter and a third of disputes concerned wages. This is similar to the 'all industry' average for the years 1975–78 (ABS Catalogue no.6322.0) but much less than the corresponding 'all industry' figure for Great Britain (Department of Employment Gazette, June 1976–79).[2] This suggests the influence of National Wage Indexation, which was operating in the former, but not in the latter, country. We do not need to repeat the wage indexation argument, since it was spelt out in Chapter Two (p.47). However, it is significant that the settlement of wages above workplace level and the related control of wage drift is reinforced by tight industry-wide awards and agreements. Accordingly, the most important construction and ship-building awards and agreements are of the paid rates type, that is, they prohibit *inter alia* wage increases stemming from workplace bargaining. The waterfront accommodation structure also closely regulates wage increases by means of an industry-wide award supplemented by formal workplace (port-wide) agreements.

The evidence presented above suggests that centralisation and formalisation of pay settlements (when these are based on substantial agreement between the parties) are conducive to a comparatively low level of pay disputes .This argument gains support from the Telecom case, where pay is centrally determined. But the exceptionally low incidence of conflicts over pay in this industry is probably the result of particularly generous wage increases gained by Telecom employees (and other civil servants) during the years of the Whitlam Labor Government (1972–75).

The large number of conflicts over management policy and behaviour in three of our four industries stems from the way in which the conciliation and arbitration system reinforces conservative values, which protect managerial prerogatives. As we have mentioned previously, unions have no legal right under the Federal system to negotiate on issues such as hiring, transfers, work effort, technological change, access to information, investment decisions, and much else besides. Moreover, despite the efforts of some of the tribunal members, there is no general legal encouragement to negotiate at workplace level. Under these restrictive circumstances management are not required to manage by consent, so the only way most workers can protect their interests is by taking industrial action. In short, the narrow scope of joint regulation encourages the use of sanctions in order to force management to recognise workers' job property rights (Turner *et al.*, 1967: 336–339). This is especially relevant to such issues as dismissals, lay-offs, and technological change, all of which touch on workers' central work problems: employment instability and job control.

This argument, based on the scope of accommodation structures, is supported by an analysis of the waterfront industry, which, with only a small proportion of disputes attributable to managerial issues is the exception (p.93). Here we find that a representative statutory body, the WIC, 'performs many functions that in other industries would be undertaken by the employer' (p.95). This includes the contentious areas of engagement and allocation of labour. Turkington (1976: 307) suggests that, on balance, the WIC has had an ameliorative effect on industrial conflict. As far as management issues are concerned, one might go further and conclude that this body has a very significant moderating effect, indicated by comparison with industries where management's traditional rights are legally protected.

In considering trade union issues, we shall omit intra-union communication matters (see Table 6.1) from our discussion, since these refer to stop-work meetings, which have already been examined (pp.149–50). This leaves demarcation disputes as a common source of conflict in all but the telecommunications industry.

The reasons for these disputes are to be found mainly in the conjunction of an occupational union structure and changes in technology and materials. Occupational unionism fosters job territory consciousness among workers, since relinquishment of an occupational terrain may mean unemployment for the worker, and a precedent that may entail a large loss of union membership to another organisation. Job boundaries are, therefore, jealously guarded by members and union officials alike, but inevitably technological change poses critical problems of job definition, bringing unions into conflict with one another. This is most apparent in shipbuilding but is also a feature of the construction and waterfront industries.

The tribunals have legal jurisdiction over many, though not all, demarcation disputes but unions are generallly unwilling to submit themselves to arbitration on the grounds that unfavourable precedents might be established. Factionalism appears to be associated with many of these disputes, and it is perhaps because of this that tribunals have not been very successful in preventing and resolving these problems. With the exception of the BTG, inter-union bodies have not done much better, possibly for the same reasons.

Why are demarcation conflicts so rare among the Telecom unions, despite the same conjunction of occupational unionism and rapid technological change? The answer lies in the particular structure of occupations in Telecom and the *direction* of change. Unlike construction and shipbuilding, the occupations in Telecom are highly distinguishable, both in terms of tasks and in relation to the work areas in which the various skill groups are employed. Moreover, technological change has not, at least up to now, generated alterations in work practices that call these distinctions into question. This is largely on account of the nature of the new technology, but also because management is particularly sensitive to the probable adverse consequences of introducing change that would lead to antagonisms of this kind. Thus the Telecom case suggests that technological change and occupational unionism do not inevitably lead to a high incidence of demarcation disputes.

The next question to be discussed is that of strike duration. Certain common denominators of three factors — workers' power, accommodation structure, and trade union behaviour — provide the main explanations for the short duration of most disputes.

The bargaining power of workers in the four industries has already been explored (pp.138–40), here it is only necessary to add that this capacity to impose substantial costs on the business enterprise typically evokes a more rapid response from management than in most other industries. This is where the accommodation structure becomes important: employers can apply for a hearing by a tribunal, which, in the event of an industrial dispute, is rarely refused. Indeed the tribunals pride themselves on the speed with which they deal with industrial problems. This same point is stressed in the discussion of the waterfront, with its somewhat different accommodation system (p.100).

Divided along occupational lines, and lacking a unified control system, Australian unions are generally fragmented and weak. Furthermore, for historical reasons associated with the lack of professionalism in trade union affairs, and inter-union competition, these labour organisations extract very low dues from their members (Wielgosz, 1974). As they have to fight on many industrial and regional fronts, Australian unions are ill-equipped to engage in lengthy struggles. Fortunately, they are rarely called on to do so by their members, for whom it has become customary to engage in conflict without serious thought being given to strategy and discipline. Australian workers are not accustomed to the kind of industrial warfare which has characterised much of American labour history (Brecher, 1972; Taft and Ross, 1969: 281–395). Apart from a small number of campaign actions, most disputes, both in the industries under review and more generally, exhibit a certain sparkplug quality: a rapid upsurge of anger coupled with demands for betterment and swift application of sanctions. After a short interval, with tempers cooled, union officials are engaged in settling the dispute and encouraging a resumption of work. Even campaign struggles (typically in support of new industry-wide awards) take the form of large scale, short duration demonstrations. These are not simply tactical responses to conciliation and arbitration proceedings, they indicate material and organisational deficiencies in union resources.

The use of bans, and indeed other tactics short of a strike, may be expected to flourish in a context where large scale trials of strength are discouraged. The considerably longer average duration of bans in the four industries suggests, as has been argued previously, (pp.109ff.) that these forms of sanction are generally less disruptive and can, therefore, be endured by management for a longer period.

The final dimension of industrial action to which we now turn concerns intra-industry variations in union militancy. With the exception of the waterfront, which is almost totally dominated by eighteen port-wide unions covering the same occupation, the type and frequency of industrial action has been shown to vary considerably between unions in the same industry. We shall argue that this is explained by factors associated with the mode of production and union structure and character. The concept of power provides the key to understanding the relationship between these elements.

For analytical purposes a clear distinction must be made between two aspects of power: strategic position in the division of labour and organisational resources. The first dimension confers certain objective advantages or disadvantages on particular occupational or union groups; these are often synonymous, given the preponderance of occupational unionism. The second aspect refers to persons and material objects (e.g. union organisation, money, communications technology,) that might be developed to facilitate industrial struggle. Thus the distribution of organisational resources between work groups will influence their capacity and willingness to engage in industrial action. In practice the two factors are likely to be dialectically related: a favourable strategic position will tend to attract organisational resources capable of ensuring that this potential is realised, while the presence of organisational resources, for example, a trade union, will encourage a search for the most favourable strategic position in the division of labour in which workers might be mobilised to improve their standards and status.

This interplay of factors bearing on the distribution of power will now be examined by reference to specific union groups which are at the two extremes of the industrial action spectrum in the three industries. These are presented in Table 6.4.

TABLE 6.4

Participation in industrial action by selected occupations and unions in three industries.

Industry	Industrial action			
	High level of participation		Low level of participation	
	Occupations	Unions	Occupations	Unions
Construction	Labourers	BLF	Painters	OPDU
			Plasterers	Plasterers
			Bricklayers	BWIU
Shipbuilding	Ships' painters and dockers	FSPDU	Tradesmen's assistants	FIA
Telecom	Technicians	ATEA	Clerks	APSA, ACOA
			Linesmen	APTU

Source: Industry case studies.

The industry studies demonstrate that construction labourers and Telecom technicians occupy strategic positions in their respective industries. This is less apparent in the case of the ships' painters and dockers, whom we shall discuss shortly. For the moment, it is helpful to highlight the organisational attributes of conflict evidenced by the occupational groups referred to immediately above.

Although labourers frequently engage in autonomous conflicts, they are almost as likely to be involved in domestic struggles and are often at the forefront of the much less common single union award campaigns (p.50). Ships' painters and dockers also engage in domestic disputes, but, like the Telecom technicians (p.111), most of their struggles are of the autonomous type (p.73). The common emphasis on single union disputes confined to one workplace rather than several, and instigated at establishment level, is related to similarities in union structure, accommodation arrangements, and the availability or otherwise of organisational resources.

Although builders' labourers tend to be poorly serviced by their union officials (p.52), these workers are encouraged to undertake unilateral direct action. This implies that most of their struggles will be of the autonomous type, especially since the labourers are party to a separate award. Depending on their relationships with other workers they will also engage in domestic conflicts. Ships' painters and dockers and the Telecom technicians are similarly covered by separate awards, while the FSPDU and ATEA, like the BLF, are confined to specific occupations within a single industry. This stimulates a high level of job consciousness. Unlike the BLF, but similar to the waterfront, the officials in these two industries are easily accessible and, indeed, are involved at an early stage in disputes.

This brief reference to organisational resources provides a clue to explaining the high incidence of disputes involving the ships' painters and dockers. Though members of this union possess considerable bargaining power at specific intervals in the production cycle, in the main their power derives from the highly cohesive organisation that characterises this union. This is based on homogeneous work groups, kin and community networks, and possibly certain commercial ventures, all of which reinforce the strong internal union control that the union officials exercise in relation to the members. The FSPDU is certainly one of the most solidaristic and exclusive unions in Australia.

A glance at the comparatively dispute-free occupations on the right side of Table 6.4, suggests that unfavourable strategic position is the most likely factor inhibiting industrial action. However, this is not the sole reason: clerks (APSA and ACOA) and linesmen (APTU) are disadvantaged by their inability to interrupt the communications network, but their weakness also stems from inadequate organisational resources. The three unions remain highly dependent on management, and, despite signs of change, continue to play the traditional minor role assigned to them (p.116). Their strategic power remains largely untapped.

Painters, plasterers, and bricklayers are capable of halting construction projects, but these workers rarely engage in industrial action. In this case, organisational deficiencies are related to particular aspects of the labour process.

Owing to changes in construction methods, tools, and materials, most work undertaken by members of these occupations can be executed adequately with techniques learnt reasonably quickly at the workplace. Given the small quantity of painting, plastering, and bricklaying on even the largest projects, these workers are generally employed in very small groups. This combination of de-skilled, small scale, and short duration employment makes it virtually impossible for the unions to control the labour supply and enforce a closed shop throughout the industry. The implication here is that, without support from other unions, any industrial action taken by these workers is likely to be thwarted by replacement of union labour with non-union workers. This contrasts with labourers, who constitute a large proportion of workers on-site and whose employment is of longer duration.

On large construction sites all workers are required to be union members. But painters, plasterers, and bricklayers show little commitment to trade unionism since much of their time is spent on smaller sites, where, as contract workers, they negotiate a price for their work independent of the unions. When employed on large sites, they arrive at the workplace generally after the major struggles have been fought. These workers, in effect, come into situations where allowances have been gained through over-award bargaining, so they do not expect to engage in industrial action.

It is hardly surprising that the aforementioned structural factors making for a dearth of motivational and organisational resources at workplace level will have an adverse effect on the unions attempting to organise these workers. It is notable that the bricklayers' union amalgamated with the carpenters some years ago; the Plasterers have a *de facto* amalgamation arrangement with the BWIU; and the Painters' union officials are continuing to try to effect a merger with the latter unions (p.57). These trends indicate organisational weakness, which simply reinforces the point made a little earlier: frequent industrial action is unlikely to occur where workers lack organisational resources, even though, technically, it would be possible to interrupt production.

The discussion of the tradesmen's assistants in the shipbuilding industry has been left until last because this example highlights the way in which trade union norms and politics may influence the distribution of organisational resources. But first, a brief inquiry into the strategic position of these workers.

While it would be possible for tradesmen to work without assistants, their productivity would be severely impaired, thereby adversely affecting the maintenance of ships and equipment. But this would not have an immediate effect. Thus in terms of strategic position the tradesmen's assistants are not very powerful, but they are not technically weak either. Far more important, however, is the norm that tradesmen will not generally work without assistants, nor will they permit non-union labour to undertake these tasks. So in practice the tradesmen's assistants apparently have quite considerable power. But this conclusion would be premature for two reasons: they might incur the displeasure of tradesmen whose ability to work would be affected, or they would invite the intervention of the Painters and Dockers union (FSPDU) whose members would be eager to claim this unskilled work, some of which is within their legal jurisdiction, or both. These are important factors that tend to restrict the participation of tradesmen's assistants in industrial action, except as part of wider struggles, that is, in domestic or campaign type conflicts where the two aforementioned dangers are absent (see p.73 and p.81).

There is another significant factor that accounts for the tradesmen's assistants' weakness and consequent low participation in single union disputes. We refer here to the lack of official union emphasis on the development of shop stewards. The FIA is one of the largest right wing unions in Australia. Wary of shop stewards and shop committees, since these are likely to be 'captured' by left wing elements, the FIA union officials do not encourage workplace organisation. Indeed, in shipbuilding, FIA members are often isolated, since in practice shop committees are dominated by left wing unions such as the AMWSU, BWIU, FEDFA, FMWU, and FSPDU. This intensifies FIA officials' fears of losing work and members in the industry. It also means that the tradesmen's assistants have even fewer resources available to ensure success in disputes with management. But this analysis should not be construed as implying that it is impossible to create the necessary resources: at one large yard the FIA stewards take a leading role on the shop committee and have consequently been able to develop substantial resources independent of the official union. This has resulted in the FIA members gaining the reputation of being the most militant workers at that establishment.

To sum up on the question of variations in union militancy: there are few occupations whose strategic position in the division of labour confers so much, or so little, power that organisational resources are an insignificant factor in determining the distribution of power between labour and capital. Our analysis shows that the groups most frequently involved in industrial action possess a favourable strategic position *and* sufficient organisational resources to restrict access to these jobs by non-union labour. The ships' painters and dockers case illustrates how organisational resources can supplement or even, to some extent, substitute for power deriving from strategic position. The least dispute-prone groups tend to possess less strategic power and inadequate organisational resources, although the discussion of the tradesmen's assistants showed that these are not necessarily related in this way. Our general conclusion is that, where strategic position is favourable, resources need not be substantial to facilitate frequent resort to industrial action. Neither is it inevitable that strong union organisation will develop, given an advantageous strategic position, although this is likely where other adverse factors are absent or insignificant. Where strategic position is less beneficial, organisational resources may or may not be acquired, depending on the existence of relevant structural factors and the strategies of the union leadership.

Finally, our analysis implies that variations in union militancy cannot be properly understood without analysing the interplay between the strategic position of the many different occupational groups that are covered by the relevant labour organisations and the resources that permit successful mobilisation.

Concluding Comments: Research and Policy Implications

This project was designed to provide a more theoretical basis for one important aspect of Australian industrial relations. The initial idea, sketched in the first chapter, was to create a framework that would encourage empirical research and lead towards a better understanding of industrial action. The results of our industry case studies were reported in Chapters Two to Five, and the final chapter has concentrated on developing a theory based on the aforementioned materials. While our theory should be regarded as no more than a starting point, much of the foregoing analysis should be relevant outside the Australian context. This final section will be directed towards exploring some of these possibilities, in order that the theory may be tested and elaborated. To begin with, several conceptual issues will be raised, thereafter questions of research strategy will be considered. Methodological problems will be excluded from the subsequent discussion; these are left to future researchers better able to assess the research terrain in the light of access and resource constraints.

Our theoretical scheme raises at least four problems that require further examination. These may be briefly described as misconceptualisation, underconceptualisation, overconceptualisation, and inadequate conceptual linkage. Each issue will be addressed in turn.

As an example of the first problem, the notion of mode of production encompasses several concepts (*viz.* markets, ownership, control, technology, and labour process), whose theoretical unity is perhaps less obvious than might first appear. It may, therefore, be better to conceptualise these aspects separately or combine only some of them, although this might only serve to change the meaning of what is essentially a critical concept (Horton, 1964).

With regard to the problem of underconceptualisation, there are several key ideas that could be elaborated in more detail. For example, workers' discontent may be analysed further, perhaps with the aid of psychological concepts, in order to distinguish between various types of discontent. Likewise, a more precise definition of various forms of power is certainly quite feasible. Moreover, as the theory stands at present, the state remains underconceptualised, as do the employers and their strategies.

Other concepts, such as accommodation structure, are perhaps too cumbersome: it may be possible to simplify the notion in this case, for example, by discarding certain dimensions which have little or no explanatory value. Finally, additional theorising that focuses on the relationships between the concepts may be useful in pinpointing areas that might be worth pursuing in further empirical enquiries. For example, what further relationships are there between the mode of production and union structure? This is clearly a question of crucial relevance to the power of the labour movement and its ability to engage in industrial action.

Assuming that conceptual improvements can be effected, in what direction might research usefully be pursued? There are at least two non-mutually exclusive possibilities: firstly, the conduct of further theoretically informed industry level studies and, secondly, projects that utilise different units of analysis undertaken at higher or lower levels of abstraction.

More work of the kind reported in this volume would need to aim at testing presumed relationships and developing more precise hypotheses. It may be possible to examine industries characterised by a similar accommodation structure but whose mode of production or trade union structure and character or both are quite different. This would imply a comparison between different industries in the same society (see Moore, 1979: 227–269). On the other hand, it may prove fruitful to investigate industries of the same kind in advanced capitalist economies but under different institutional conditions. This would mean international comparisons of industrial action in similar industries.

There are other interesting research paths within this comparative industry framework. For example, an approach that includes analysis of industrial action in the same industry, but at varying historical junctures,would be a particularly rewarding exercise in countries that have experienced a fundamental change in institutional arrangements. To round off this part of the discussion, there is also the opportunity of analysing the stability and changes in industrial action patterns over time. This type of study would help to illuminate the long run dynamic relationships between the key factors.

The second direction in which research might proceed is by using alternative units of analysis at varying levels of abstraction. At present, for example, Frenkel and Coolican are engaged on a project focusing on comparative union behaviour. Other useful research at the work group and plant level has been undertaken and could be extended, compared, and integrated with industry level studies. Similarly, there is no reason why international comparisons of industrial disputes cannot draw upon and contribute towards improvements in theory at the industrial level. Finally, if a comprehensive theory of industrial conflict is to be forged at any level of abstraction, studies of collective action will need to be integrated with work on individual and unorganised expressions of discontent (Edwards, 1979).

From theory we turn our attention to practice. For those searching for a simple solution to the 'industrial action problem' there is little comfort to be found here, for industrial relations are too complex to admit the kinds of 'multi-disciplinary packages' so dear to the hearts of management consultants. Indeed, one might argue that industrial action should not be evaluated in isolation: it is only one symptom of what might be termed the industrial relations climate of an industry, enterprise, or workplace. What management and unions should perhaps be thinking of is the development of a set of criteria by which the quality of industrial relations can be regularly monitored and assessed. These results could play some part in subsequent movements in pay, conditions, and benefits at the workplace or enterprise level.

If, in the interim, custom and the law ensure that industrial action continues to be considered as a separate issue, our analysis suggests that it is impossible to elicit any policy implications without the parties first specifying goals of a realistic rather than idealistic kind. If management were to say: 'we value industrial peace and our aim is to secure this objective' it could be argued that such a position is, at least in respect of many industries, quite untenable. Instead, the parties would do better to assess the kind of long term relationships they prefer to have with one another and, given the inevitability of conflict, the patterns of industrial action most likely to serve their interests. Our impression is that 'the problem of industrial action' has rarely been approached in this explicit manner, let alone formed the basis for long term negotiations.

The case studies indicate the powerful influence that accommodation structures, various aspects of the mode of production, and union organisation and structure exert on patterns of industrial action. It is also clear that these variables are interdependent, so that a change in one is likely to lead to changes in the others. While not enough is known about these interrelationships, the parties would be ill-advised to consider the reform of industrial relations by concentrating on one aspect without evaluating the effects on the other variables. Unfortunately, much recent discussion concerning 'problems' of worker participation, union amalgamation, and rationalisation of accommodation structures fails to take a sufficiently comprehensive and systematic view of industrial relations. Rarely, too, do such proposals focus on a particular industry: it is too often assumed that different industrial sectors have similar requirements. Paradoxically, our research indicates that many common problems are caused by the imposition of institutions and procedures insufficiently tailored to the deprivations and demands of particular groups of managers and workers.

At this final point, it is difficult not to resist the observation that, apart from the waterfront, joint regulation at workplace level remains rudimentary, haphazard, and informal. The relatively high incidence of autonomous and, to a lesser extent, domestic disputes are perhaps indicative of a serious syndrome in much of Australian industry. We refer here to alienation, the lack of work motivation, and inefficient work practices; these are applicable to management and workers alike (Sinclair, 1979). This situation is unlikely to be improved by piecemeal change, for the problems appear to be deeply rooted in the economic and industrial relations infrastructure. They have, over time, also encouraged certain cultural responses that cannot be changed over a short period and by minor adjustments.

Fragmented unions and employers associations are not conducive to long term bargaining, and, perhaps because of this, a traditionally interventionist state has been largely responsible for accommodation structures that regulate, but fail to motivate, management and workers. It may well be time for a thorough, large scale investigation of industrial relations in Australia so that the quality of debate and policy can be raised to a level commensurate with the challenge the country faces in the 1980s.

NOTES

1.   An informal norm among lower line managers facilitates managerial discretion regarding the recording of stop-work meetings. Where management believe these meetings will contribute to dispute resolution, deduction for time away from work is waived.
2.   On an annual average basis, pay disputes accounted for 26.3 per cent and 55.1 per cent of the relevant totals in Australia and Great Britain respectively.

Bibliography

Aldridge, A. (1976): *Power, Authority and Restrictive Practices*, Basil Blackwell, Oxford.

Alexander, K. J. W. & Jenkins, C.L. (1970): *Fairfields: a study of industrial change*, Allen Lane, London.

Argyris, C., (1964): *Integrating the Individual and the Organisation*, Wiley and Son, New York.

Aungles, S. & Szelenyi, I. (1979): 'Structural conflicts between the state, local government and monopoly capital – the case of Whyalla in South Australia,' *Australian and New Zealand Journal of Sociology*, vol. 15, no.1.

Australia and New Zealand Bank (1978): *Surveys of Construction Activity* (Quarterly).

Australian Conciliation and Arbitration Commission (April 1975): *National Wage Case Decision.*

Australian Conciliation and Arbitration Commission (September 1978): *Wage Fixation Principles Decision.*

Australian Public Service, *Australian Public Service Position Classification Standards*, AGPS, no date.

Bassett, M. (1972) *Confrontation '51: The 1951 Waterfront Dispute*, Reeds, Wellington.

Batstone, E., Boraston, I. & Frenkel, S. (1977): *Shop Stewards in Action*, Basil Blackwell, Oxford.

Batstone, E., Boraston, I. & Frenkel, S. (1978): *The Social Organisation of Strikes*, Basil Blackwell, Oxford.

Bendix, R. (1974): *Work and Authority in Industry*, University of California Press, Berkeley.

Beynon, H. (1973): *Working for Ford*, Penguin, Harmondsworth.

Boraston, I., Clegg, H. & Rimmer, M. (1975): *Workplace and Union*, Heinemann, London.

Brecher, J. (1972): *Strike!*, Straight Arrow Books, San Francisco.

Brown, R. K., Bannen, P., Cousins, J. M. & Samphier, M. L. (1972): 'The contours of solidarity: social stratification and industrial relations in shipbuilding', *British Journal of Industrial Relations*, vol. 10, no.1.

Brown, W. A. (1973): *Piecework Bargaining*, Heinemann, London.

Builders Labourers Federation Journal (1979): no.3.

Burns, T. & Stalker, G. M. (1961): *The Management of Innovation*, Tavistock Publications, London.

Cameron, G. C. (1964): 'Post war strikes in the North East shipbuilding and ship repairing industry, 1946–61', *British Journal of Industrial Relations*, vol. 2, no.1.

Chamberlain N. W. & Kuhn J. W. (1965): *Collective Bargaining*, 2nd edn, McGraw Hill, New York.

Clegg, H. (1976): *Trade Unionism under Collective Bargaining*, Basil Blackwell, Oxford.

Clegg, H. A. (1979): *The Changing System of Industrial Relations in Great Britain*, Basil Blackwell, Oxford.

Commission on Industrial Relations (1971): *Report no. 22, Shipbuilding and Shiprepairing*, HMSO, London.

Commission of Inquiry into the Nature and Terms of Employment in the New South Wales Housing Industry, (Chairman G. A. Burns), 1979–1980.

Committee of Enquiry into Industrial Relations in Naval Dockyards (1975): *Final report*, Presented to the Minister of Defence, 10 November 1975, mimeo.

Cordell, J. (1979): 'Tendering – who pays?,' *The Builder NSW*, Sept.

Cordell's *Quarterly Review of Construction in New South Wales & ACT.*

Cousins, J. & Brown, R. K. (1975): 'Patterns of paradox: shipbuilding workers' images of society,' in M. Bulmer (ed.), *Working-Class Images of Society*, Routledge and Kegan Paul, London.

163

Crouch, C. (1977): *Class Conflict and the Industrial Relations Crisis.*

Cruise, H. F. (1957): *Productivity and Progress,* Australian Institute of Political Science, Angus and Robertson, Sydney, Heinemann, London.

Dubin, R. (1956): 'Industrial Workers' Worlds: A study of the "Central Life Interests" of Industrial Workers', *Social Problems,* vol. 3, pp.131–42.

Edwards, P. K. (1977): 'A Critique of the Kerr-Siegal Hypothesis of Strikes and the Isolated Mass: A Study of the Falsification of Sociological Knowledge', *The Sociological Review,* vol. 25, no.3, New Series, pp.551–74.

Edwards, P. K. (1979): 'Strikes and Unorganised Conflict: 'Some Further Considerations', *British Journal of Industrial Relat'ons,* vol. 17, no. 1, pp.95–103.

Eisele, C. F. (1974): 'Organisation Size, Technology, and Frequency of Strikes', *Industrial and Labor Relations Review,* vol. 27, no.4, pp.560–71.

Eldridge, J. E. T. (1968): 'The demarcation dispute in the shipbuilding industry, in *Industrial Disputes,* Routledge and Kegan Paul, London.

Flanders, A. (1970): *Management and Unions,* Faber and Faber, London.

Foster, H. G. (1978): 'Industrial Relations in Construction: 1970–1977', *Industrial Relations,* vol. 17, no. 1.

Fox, A. (1966): *Industrial Sociology and Industrial Relations,* Research Paper no. 3, Royal Commission on Trade Unions and Employers' Associations, HMSO, London.

Fox, A. (1971): *A Sociology of Work in Industry,* Collier Macmillan, London.

Fox, A. (1974): *Beyond Contract: Work, Power and Trust Relations,* Faber and Faber, London.

Fox, A. & Flanders, A. (1969): "Collective Bargaining: From Donovan to Durkheim" in Flanders, A. *Management and Unions,* Faber and Faber, London.

Frenkel, S. J. (1978a): 'Industrial Conflict, workplace characteristics and accommodation structure in the Pilbara iron ore industry,' *Journal of Industrial Relations,* vol. 20, no.4.

Frenkel, S. J. (1978b): "The 'Causes' of Strikes: a Preliminary analysis of Australian Employer and Union Officials' perceptions," Department of Industrial Relations, Working Paper, University of New South Wales.

Frenkel, S. J. (1978c): 'Towards a Theory of Strikes in Australia', Department of Industrial Relations Working Paper, University of New South Wales.

Frenkel, S. J. (1979): Explorations in Industrial Conflict: the New South Wales Coal Industry, Department of Industrial Relations, Working Paper, University of New South Wales.

Frenkel, S. J. (1980): Inter-Industry Strike Patterns: Towards A New Analytical Framework, *Australian Journal of Management,* vol. 5, no. 1.

Frenkel, S. J. and Coolican, A. (1979): 'Industrial Struggle: New Directions in Social Research' *New Zealand Journal of Industrial Relations,* vol. 4. no. 3.

Friedman, A. (1976): 'Union Structure and Rank and File Revolt', *Industrial Relations,* vol. 31, no. 2, pp. 261–82.

Friedman, A. L. (1977): *Industry and Labour: Class Struggle at Work and Monopoly Capitalism,* Macmillan, London.

Gallie, D. (1978): *In search of the new working class: Automation and social integration within the capitalist enterprise,* Cambridge University Press, Cambridge.

Goldthorpe, J. H., Lockwood, D., Bechhofer, F. & Platt, J. (1968): *The Affluent Worker: Industrial Attitudes and Behaviour,* Cambridge University Press, Cambridge.

Goodrich, C. L. (1975): *The Frontier of Control,* Pluto Press, London.

Haraszti, M. (1977): *A Worker in a Worker's State,* Penguin, Harmondsworth.

Harrowfield, J. D. (1978): *Trade Union Amalgamation in the Building Industry,* University of Melbourne, unpublished Masters Thesis.

Haskall, M. A. (1977): "Green   s: Worker Control and the Urban Environment," *Industrial Relations,* vol. 16, no. 2, pp. 205–14.

Hewitt, J. (1979): 'Address by Jimmy Hewitt to Waterside Workers' Federation of Australia', *Port News* (Journal of the Auckland Waterside Workers' Union), November, pp. 21–5.

Holden, W. S. (1967): 'The Anatomy of Two Newspaper Industrial Disputes: US and Australia, *Journal of Industrial Relations*, vol. 9, no. 1, pp. 1–11.

Horton, J. (1964): 'The dehumanisation of anomie and alienation', *British Journal of Sociology*, vol. 15, no. 4.

Howard, W. A. (1977) 'Australian trade unions in the context of union theory', *Journal of Industrial Relations* vol. 19, no. 3.

Hyman, R. & Fryer, R. H. (1977): 'Trade Unions: Sociology and Political Economy', in T. Clarke & L. Clements (eds): *Trade Unions under Capitalism*, Fontana, Glasgow.

Hyman, R. (1978): 'Occupational structure, collective organisation and industrial militancy', in C. Crouch & A. Pizzorno (eds), *The Resurgence of Class Conflict in Western Europe Since 1968*, vol. 2, Macmillan, London.

Industrial Registrar under The Trade Union Act, 1881, (1976): *Report of The Industrial Registrar*, Sydney, No. 312.

Industries Assistance Commission (1976): *Shipbuilding*, 20 September, 1976, AGPS, Canberra.

Ingham, G. K. (1974): *Strikes and Industrial Conflict*, Macmillan, London.

Isaac, J. E. & Ford, G. W. (eds) 1971: *Australian Labour Relations: Readings*, 2nd edn, Sun Books, Melbourne.

Interim Report of the Inquiry into Employment in the Building Industry, (The Evatt Report) (1975): mimeo.

Jackson, P. & Sisson, K. (1976): 'Employers' Confederations in Sweden and the U.K. and the significance of Industrial Infrastructure', *British Journal of Industrial Relations*, vol. 14, no. 3, pp. 306–23.

Jansen, S., Thompson, C. & Zantis C. (1978): 'Communication in Telecom between Staff and Management', unpublished paper, Queensland University.

Korpi, W. (1978): *The Working Class in Welfare Capitalism*, Routledge and Kegan Paul, London.

Korpi, W. & Shalev, M. (1979): 'Strikes, Industrial Relations and Class Conflict in Capitalist Societies', *British Journal of Sociology*, vol. 30, no. 2, pp. 164–87.

Levinson, H. M. (1966): 'Wage Determination Under Collective Bargaining', in A. Flanders (ed.): *Collective Bargaining*, Penguin, Harmondsworth.

Lipsky, D. B. & Farber, H. S. (1976): 'The Composition of Strike Activity in the Construction Industry', *Industrial and Labor Relations Review*, vol. 29, no. 3.

Lloyd's Register of Shipping (1979): *Annual Report, 1978*. Lloyd's Register, London.

Lockwood, D. (1966): 'Sources of variation in working-class images of society', *Sociological Review, vol. 14, no. 2.*

Lovell, K. (1979): 'Industrial Relations in the Building Industry, Current Problems, Future Trends', a paper presented at the School of Building, Industrial Relations Seminar, University of New South Wales, 28–29 September 1979.

Low-Beer, J. R. (1978): *Protest and Participation*, Cambridge University Press, Cambridge.

Macken, J. J. (1974): *Australian Industrial Laws: The Constitutional Basis*, Law Book Company, Sydney.

McLean, R. A. (1979): 'Interindustry Differences in Strike Activity', *Industrial Relations*, vol. 18, no. 1, pp. 103–9.

Mallet, S. (1975): *The New Working Class*, Spokesman Books, Nottingham.

Martin, R. M. (1975): *Trade Unions in Australia*, Penguin, Ringwood.

Mills, C. W. (1948): *The New Men of Power*, Harcourt Brace, New York.

Mills, C. Wright (1963): 'Situated Action and Vocabularies of Motive' in I. L. Horowitz (ed.), *Power, Politics and People*, Free Press, New York.

Mitchell, R. (1979): 'Industrial Relations Under a Conservative Government: The Coalition's Labour Law Programme 1975 to 1978.' *Journal of Industrial Relations*, vol. 21. no. 4.

Moore, Barrington Jnr, (1978): *Injustice: the social bases of obedience and revolt*, Macmillan, London.

New South Wales Corporate Affairs Commission, (1978): *Annual Report*, Sydney.

Oxnam, D. W. (1966): 'The incidence of strikes in Australia' in J. E. Isaac and G. W. Ford (eds), *Australian Labour Relations: Readings*, 2nd edn, Sun Books, Melbourne.

Parkin, F. (1971): *Class Inequality and Political Order*, MacGibbon and Kee, London.

Parkinson, J. R. (1960): *The Economics of Shipbuilding in the United Kingdom*, Cambridge University Press, Cambridge.

Plowman, D. (1978): 'Employers Associations: Challenges and Responses', *Journal of Industrial Relations*, vol. 20, no. 3.

Plowman, D. (1979): 'National Wage Determination in 1978', *Journal of Industrial Relations*, vol. 21, no. 1.

Rawson, D. W. (1978): *Unions and Unionists in Australia*, George Allen & Unwin, Sydney.

Review Team 2 (1975): *Organisation of Technicians Districts*, mimeo.

Rimmer, M. and Sutcliffe, P. (1979): 'Slaves to Our Own Apathy: The Growth and Decline of the Shop Committee Movement in Australia, Research Report no. 4, *Business Research Centre, North Brisbane College of Advanced Education*, 1979.

Roberts, G. (1967): *Demarcation Rules in Shipbuilding and Ship Repairing* Cambridge University Press, Cambridge.

Roddewig, R. (1978): *Green Bans: the Birth of Australian Environment Politics*, Hale & Iremonger, Sydney.

Roomkin, M. (1976): 'Union Structure, Internal Control, and Strike Activity', *Industrial and Labor Relations Review*, vol. 29, no. 1, pp. 198–217.

Royal Commission into Alleged Payments to Maritime Unions (1976): *Final Report*, AGPS, Canberra.

Royal Commission of Inquiry (1972): *Report of the Royal Commission on Containers*, Government Printer, Wellington.

Salaman, G. (1974): *Community and Occupation*, Cambridge University Press, Cambridge.

Sheridan, T. (1975): *Mindful Militants: The Amalgamated Engineering Union in Australia, 1920–1972*, Cambridge University Press, Cambridge.

Shorey, J. (1976): 'An Inter-industry Analysis of Strike Frequency', *Economica*, vol. 43, no. 172, pp.349–365.

Shorter, E. & Tilly, C. (1974): *Strikes in France 1830–1968*, Cambridge University Press, Cambridge.

Sinclair, G. (1979): *I Only Work Here*, Holt, Rinehart and Winston, Sydney.

Smith, C. T. B., Clifton, R., Makeham, P., Creigh S. W. & Burn, R. V. (1978): *Strikes in Britain*, Manpower Paper no. 15, HMSO.

Socialist Party of Australia (1977): *Six Turbulent Years*, Building Industry Branch of the Socialist Party of Australia.

Sorrell, G. H. (1979): *Law in Labour Relations: An Australian Essay*, Law Book Company.

Soskice, D. (1978): 'Strike Waves and Wage Explosions, 1968–1970,' in C. Crouch and A. Pizzorno (eds), *The Resurgence of Class Conflict in Western Europe*. since 1968, vol. 2, Macmillan, London.

Stearns, P. N. (1971): *Revolutionary Syndicalism and French Labor: A Cause without Rebels*, Rutgers University Press, New Brunswick.

Stinchcombe, A. L. (1959): 'Bureaucratic and craft administration of production: a comparative study', *Administrative Science Quarterly*, vol. 4, no. 2.

Strinati, D. (1979): 'Capitalism, the State and Industrial Relations', in C. Crouch (ed.): *State and Economy in Contemporary Capitalism*, Croom Helm, London.

Sykes, A. J. M. (1967): 'The Cohesion of a trade union workshop organisation', *Sociology*, vol. 1. no. 2.

Taft, P. & Ross, P. (1969): 'American Labor Violence: Its Causes, Character, and Outcome', in H. D. Graham & T. R. Gurr, (eds): *Violence in America: Historical and Comparative Perspectives*, Signet, New American Library, New York.

Tariff Board Report (1971): *Shipbuilding*, 25 June 1971. CGPO, Canberra.

Taylor, R. (1978): *The Fifth Estate*, Routledge and Kegan Paul, London.

Thomas, B. & Deaton, D. (1978): *Labour Shortages and Economic Analysis*, Blackwell, Oxford.

Thomas, P. (1973): *Taming the Concrete Jungle*, Quality Press, Sydney.

Turkington, D. J. (1976): *Industrial Conflict: A Study of Three New Zealand Industries*, Methuen, Wellington.

Turkington, D. J. (1977a): 'The role of trade unions in foreign policy', *New Zealand International Review*, vol. 2, no. 2, pp. 12–13.

Turkington, D. J. (1977b): 'The trend of strikes in New Zealand 1971–75', *Journal of Industrial Relations*, vol. 19, no. 3, pp. 286–95.

Turner, H. A., Clack, G. & Roberts, G. (1967): *Labour Relations in the Motor Industry*, George Allen & Unwin, London.

Turner, H. A., Roberts, G. & Roberts, D. (1977): *Management Characteristics and Labour Conflict*, Cambridge University Press, Cambridge.

US Department of Labor, Bureau of Labor Statistics (1975): *Hand Book of Labor Statistics*, Reference edition.

Webb, S. & B., (1919): *Industrial Democracy*, 2nd edition, Longmans, London.

Wielgosz, J. B. (1974): 'Financial resources of Australian trade unions,' *Journal of Industrial Relations*, vol. 16, no. 4.

Wild, R. A. (1974): *Bradstow: A Study of status, class and power in a small Australian town*, Angus and Robertson, Sydney.

Woods, N. S. (1979): 'Troubled Heritage: The Main Stream of Developments in Private Sector Industrial Relations in New Zealand 1894–1978,' Occasional Papers in Industrial Relations, no. 23, Victoria University of Wellington.

Woodward, J. (1965): *Industrial Organisation: Theory and Practice*, Oxford University Press, London.

Subject index

Author index

175